Unwin Education Books
Teaching Today: 1

History and
the History Teacher

JOHN CHAFFER
LAWRENCE TAYLOR

History and the History Teacher

JOHN CHAFFER

LAWRENCE TAYLOR

Foreword by James Porter

Principal, Berkshire College of Education

London GEORGE ALLEN & UNWIN LTD

Ruskin House   Museum Street

ISBN 0 04 371037 9 hardback
     0 04 371038 7 paperback

Printed in Great Britain
Typeset in 10 point Press Roman
by Red Lion Setters, Holborn, London

Acknowledgements

We are grateful to the publishers, whose names have been credited on the relevant pages, for permission to use the charts that appear in this book.

Foreword

It is a great pleasure to write the foreword to this contribution to the *Teaching Today* series.

As the James Committee's Report on Teacher Education and Training indicated, 'The best education and training of teachers is that which is built upon and illuminated by a growing maturity and experience.' This book by John Chaffer and Lawrence Taylor will make a particular contribution to such further education and training of teachers. Too many educational texts become locked in vague generalisations or are becalmed in detail unrelated to objectives. Also, many others have accepted the ideas of student-centred education but failed to appreciate the complex skills and knowledge needed to sustain such an enterprise. This book, along with the rest of the *Teaching Today* series, demonstrates the way in which a humane and sensitive emphasis upon the experience of student learning needs to be combined with a carefully thought out rationale for teaching the subject.

John Chaffer and Lawrence Taylor are already well known in the fields of history teaching and curriculum development. The essence of their argument is that today it has become necessary to rethink the basic questions of what history should be taught and why, and how it should be taught and how assessed. Though these are day to day practical issues for the teacher, they need to be underpinned by a lucid and persuasive theory of history teaching. It is such a synthesis that the book propounds, through its continuing reiteration of the need for teachers to be able to realise general aims in terms of classroom objectives. As the authors admit, the move towards such an objectives approach is not easy. Every chapter, however, relates theory to practice through illustration and so encourages the teacher towards both practical experiment and further research. Two issues stand out: first, the ways in which the book analyses how pupils can be introduced to the experience of the historian and, secondly, the awareness that the authors show of the implications of new and interdisciplinary approaches. It is pointed out that a wide variety of approaches makes sound educational sense when viewed within the context of an objectives approach and, indeed, that the nature of history is such that every history teacher should welcome a properly planned form of interdisciplinary or integrated study. This book, therefore, will surely encourage 'practical optimism' and a 'wider professionalism' in all those who in their working lives are involved in the teaching of history whether in school, college or university department of education. It should also be of real interest to those involved in the broad field of the humanities and to those concerned with the study of the curriculum as a whole.

Finally, it provides an excellent case study, boldly written, of the ways in which contemporary curriculum development can enable one of our central civilising disciplines to achieve new expression in the world of the school.

JAMES PORTER

Contents

Charts

Introduction

History Teaching Today

The battle is no longer to gain a place for history in the schools so much as to prevent it from being lost; and in these circumstances it is only too easy to give the impression of an academic trade union with a vested interest in ensuring that the nation's education shall be so arranged that its members can go on teaching what they have always been taught.

R.H.C. Davis (1973) 'Why Have a Historical Association', in *History,* vol. 58, no. 193, p. 238.

Is the 'Death of the Past' imminent in our schools? Such is the view not only of Professor Plumb but of many teachers. Yet the subject is so exciting that if this were to happen it would surely be a tragedy. The adult audience expands continually: publishers, film and TV producers, archaeologists and local enthusiasts have all found a public for whom history provides an endless source of fascination. The contrast lies in school. Here the last decade has witnessed a 'crisis in confidence' and endless complaints of 'history in danger'.

The immediate criticism has been of traditional presentation: 'excruciatingly dangerously dull, and, what is more, of little apparent relevance' (Price, 1968: 344). Yet, if the diagnosis was obvious, the prognosis appears only to have succeeded in establishing wider questions and new doubts. To paraphrase Pares: today the sense that the history teacher has to make of his subject is an increasingly complex one. Neither experience nor experiment has yet discovered a panacea. Indeed the new styles of presentation, such as topics and projects, and the new kinds of content, such as themes or social studies, have often lacked the coherence which underlay the traditional syllabus — resulting in a 'Steptoe and Son history, bright and attractive — but junk nonetheless'. There are three main issues being raised here:

How can such 'dullness' be overcome?
How can the content be made more 'relevant'?

And in a changing world and overcrowded curriculum:

Why teach about 'the past'?

THE ISSUES: RETHINKING AND INNOVATION WITHIN THE SUBJECT

'History is not what you thought. It is what you can remember. All other history defeats itself.' Sellars and Yeatman's acid 'compulsory preface' can still introduce the first of these issues — that the greatest challenge facing any teacher is how to make history an 'involvement' subject. In the last decade the teacher has been constantly urged to 'inject life into the dead past', or to try to establish empathy through 'imaginative involvement'. The argument for motivation has also been amplified by being extended to social ends: 'a large part of its [history's] contribution to education is that it can extend the pupil's understanding of people, their action and their motives' (Gosden and Sylvester, 1968: 4).

In all this the attraction of history is that it is above all an activity, a process for sifting out evidence from the dust heap of the past in order to understand man's achievement. Encouraged by the general support for an enquiry approach to learning: 'I do, and I understand', teachers have been led to place primary emphasis upon the teaching of 'methods, skills and techniques'. Some have even been led to claim that pupils can simulate the activities of the adult historian. The issue is whether for 'immature minds' enquiry-based approaches can ever be more than a pale reflection of the sophisticated craft of the professional?

The toneless drone of the teacher's voice, the relentless march of facts and dates, the endless note-taking — the other immediate problem for teacher and pupil alike has been, and still is, that there is simply too much 'history' to be taught or learned. Yet a central aim of history teaching has always been accepted to be the 'bestowing of a heritage' and history's most characteristic mode is narrative: 'inside every analysis there is a story struggling to get out'. So history has to be an 'information subject'; the question is to what degree must it be so? Today, communicating a 'sense of heritage' has to compete alongside wider aims: 'explaining the present', 'developing understanding of contemporary problems', 'improving international understanding', 'appreciating the timeless cultural deposits of civilisations', 'training for participant democracy'. All these now figure prominently in the goals of teaching history — as the Council of Europe Survey illustrated.[1] Selection was always a priority but 'what to select' has become increasingly difficult. Can the teacher interpret these aims 'legitimately' for history and translate them into specific terms? Can he justify the priority of the one he selects against all the others? (This is one reason why the chapter on syllabus is the longest in this short book.) Roy Wake has suggested that one way to answer such questions is to pose three others:

What information do we want about the past?
Why do we want it?
What difference would it make to us if we did not possess it?[2]

Why teach history? The last of Roy Wake's questions surely begs this further one. For the traditional syllabus it was simply assumed: 'the importance of having the outlines of every study accurately defined will be readily conceded . . . if the groundwork be traced in early life it will scarcely ever be obliterated'.[3] All recent writing, however, has argued the aim to be that of some introduction to 'historical thinking'. Most writers, however, following the contemporary emphasis on the enquiry approach, have tended to see this simply in terms of teaching 'methods, techniques and skills' and only one, Burston, has argued his meaning in terms of the 'nature' of history. Lacking their own champions, many teachers have adopted the rationale put forward by historians.[4] School teachers have always tended to look up to the universities and the fundamental issue is whether this rationale is transferable. How far is justifying the study of the subject 'for its own sake' related to the needs of schools? Are the contexts of undergraduate or postgraduate study different in principle or degree to that of the comprehensive school? There have been some signs of concern to examine the relationship between the nature of history, the activity of the historian and teaching history at the university. What has been less examined (as the opening statement argues) is the relationship between the nature of history and the purposes of teaching it in schools.

In sum, all the assumptions conventionally used to justify the teaching of history in school need to be re-examined:

whether as a *discipline*: the relation between the search for 'truth' and an 'introduction to historical thinking';
for *general and cultural education*: the relative values of purposes such as 'heritage', 'development' or 'citizenship';
and lastly, for *the personal development of the pupil*: more specific definitions of 'critical thinking' and 'imaginative involvement'.

THE CONTEMPORARY CONTEXT: OUTSIDE PRESSURES

Of course, no one of these issues is novel. Historical Association pamphlets published during 1906-11, the first five years of its existence, anticipate each of them. Again, Happold's championing of 'historical training' brought into discussion all the possible objectives of history teaching back in 1928. Even the present addiction to 'topical relevance' was reflected earlier by Gooch's *History of Our Time* of 1911, Adamson's plea for 'teaching history backwards' made in 1912 and the continuing debate on the validity of the study of contemporary history in *History* ever since 1922.[5]

The difference today is the sense in which conditions appear climacteric — the national and wider ranging debate which is making the need for change actual and real. First, since the institution of the Schools Council for Curriculum and Examinations in 1964, reform of the content of the curriculum has at last become an official focus of attention. Curriculum renewal, the rethinking and restyling of subject content in terms of an enquiry-based philosophy, had become generally accepted. Hadow's advocacy of subject disciplines as 'centres of activity and experience' is nearer reality than ever before.

Then the field of the humanities has broadened. It can be no longer regarded as restricted to the 'English subjects': English, history, geography and religious instruction. The social sciences now fill a respectable and demanded role in the curriculum at all levels, not only because of advances in knowledge but more because of the wish of contemporary society to understand itself.

Parallel with this has been the effect of comprehensive reorganisation. Despite the Black Paper criticisms, this means that subject disciplines, previously argued and developed as preparation for university work, now have to be rethought as a part of secondary education for all. As both the Newsom Report and Enquiry I brought out, such rethinking bore particularly hard on history as traditionally taught. Also the social aims of the comprehensive school have led to explicit demands that the curriculum reflect 'topical relevance', and include the study of 'significant human issues' and 'social problems'. If traditionally history was regarded as the vehicle for all such aims, in practice it was no more than a caretaker. Now, making much play with pupil criticisms, teachers of the social sciences and advocates of integration have both been making bids for the time and place of history in the school curriculum.

Lastly, the apparent security afforded by the traditional subject examination system has largely been undermined. Of course, its restricting effects upon the range and character of history teaching have always been piously lamented, but the last decade has seen more practical developments and research then ever before. The introduction of the Certificate of Secondary Education has been a powerful catalyst for change and as Lamont has warned: 'the conventional examination papers in history now face their sternest challenge' (1970: 213).

THE TEACHER'S DILEMMA

Many teachers at first reacted despairingly: 'history in danger'. However, as the dust of initial controversy and confrontation has begun to settle, the emerging contrasts are not only of uncertainty but of opportunity.

In curriculum, the English tradition has always stressed the autonomy of the school. Curriculum reform has re-emphasised this, particularly the teacher's role in decision making. If the Schools Council had a motto it would read: 'to help teachers decide what they want to teach and how they want to teach it'. Also comprehensive reorganisation has shown that all the comfortable, conventional wisdoms of subject-teaching were really 'hand-me-downs' from the university. The new situation has shown them to be essentially value-judgements rather than immutable laws. However, if independence is an attractive idea, it also carries a heavy responsibility. Teachers are already very busy people and curriculum renewal, keeping abreast of new thinking and writing about a subject, is demanding enough — as the next paragraph argues. Curriculum innovation, extending the dimensions of aim or method, is even more exacting in that it asks the teacher to see such 'renewal' in the wider context of change in education as a whole — as is argued by Hoyle below.

In the last decade there has been more writing on history teaching than ever before. But it has only seemed to compound the uncertainties. The stream of books and articles have each been primarily concerned to demonstrate the values of a particular approach, or how a method can stimulate involvement, or how the needs of a particular age and ability group can best be met. Even the important symposia edited by Burston (1972) and Ballard (1970) seem to lack any consensus or reconciliation of principles. The question facing the teacher is whether all these writings differ in principle or simply in their respective emphases.

The real challenge, as Hoyle (1973) puts it, is one of facing up to the responsibilities of 'professionalism'. Many would argue that teachers are already doing this. For history there is now a widespread network of local associations and 1969 saw the establishment of the first journal purely devoted to this field — *Teaching History*.[6] Hoyle, however, sees professionalism as meaning not only classroom competence but an 'extended' concern which sets teaching in the context of theory, research and current educational trends. It is asking the teacher to pass his knowledge and skills under continual review — is this necessary? The inspiration behind such urging is that of adjusting to the needs of a rapidly changing situation, a view officially endorsed in the recommendations of the 1972 White Paper, particularly the clauses encouraging the expansion of in-service education.[7]

The purpose of this short book is to survey the range of developments in thinking about history and history teaching, particularly since 1945. The hope is that it will help a teacher to recognise the general assumptions that inform his thinking, as well as to introduce him to the range of differing approaches — not necessarily those in his own field. Lastly, though acknowledging a situation of rapid change, it is important to add that the aim is to encourage practical optimism and so to act as an introduction to further reading and study.

NOTE ON ARRANGEMENT OF REFERENCES, FOOTNOTES AND BIBLIOGRAPHY

We have given *summary references* (author, date, page) in the body of the text when the books quoted are included in the bibliography at the end of each chapter. Otherwise, where the reference is only indirectly relevant to the theme of the chapter, *notes* are used. These are also listed at the end of each chapter. The *bibliography* is designed as a selective introduction to further reading on the material of the chapter. For those areas where there is an established literature the bibliography has been restricted to the standard works for greater clarity. Less familiar, or recently developed, aspects of the subject may appear to have been given more extensive treatment but this is because their literature is still mainly in article form. Readers who require a more comprehensive survey of the literature on any aspect of history teaching can easily build this up from John Fines (1969) *The Teaching of History in the United Kingdom* (Historical Association) and his subsequent addenda to this to be found in *Teaching History,* vol. 2, no. 6 (1971), pp. 153-7 and vol. 3, no. 9 (1974), pp. 54-9.

NOTES

1. See chapter 1 in E. H. Dance (1970).
2. See R. A. Wake (1970).
3. Ince, quoted by W. A. Lamont in Ballard (1970), p. 171.
4. The 'crisis in confidence' also affected the universities and there have been a number of notable apologia during the last ten years. These aimed to justify the value and place of the study of history in a decade which has seen many innovatory curricula, and often the devaluing of subject departments, particularly in the new regional universities.
5. See Happold (1928), Gooch (HUL, 1911), J. Adamson, *The Practice of Instruction* (London, ULP, 1912), and the following articles in *History:* R. Barker, vol. 7 (1922); R. Seton-Watson, vol. 14 (1929); G. Henderson, vol. 26 (1942); M. Beloff, vol. 30 (1946). See also *Journal of Contemporary History:* L. Woodward, vol. 1 (1966) and D. Thomson, vol. 2 (1967).
6. See numbers of *Teaching History* for lists of branches and their activities.
7. See DES (1972) *Teacher Education and Training* (James Report) (HMSO) — particularly recommendations summarised in sections 10-12 'Entitlement', 15-22 'The Establishment of Professional Centres', 26-9 'Teacher Participation in Research'.

BIBLIOGRAPHY

BALLARD, M. (ed.) (1970) *New Movements in the Study and Teaching of History* (London, Temple Smith).

BURSTON, W.H. and GREEN, C.W. (eds.) (1972) *Handbook for History Teachers* (London, Methuen, rev. edn).

DANCE, E.H. (1970) *The Place of History in Secondary Teaching: A Comparative Study* (published for the Council for Cultural Co-operation of the Council of Europe — Education in Europe, Section 2 — General and Technical Education, no. 11. London, Harrap).

GOSDEN, P.H.J.H. and SYLVESTER, D.W. (1968) *History for the Average Child* (Oxford, Blackwell).

HAPPOLD, F. (1928) *The Approach to History* (Christophers).

HOYLE, E. (1973) 'Strategies of Curriculum Change' in R. Watkins (ed.) *In-Service Training: Structure and Content* (London, Ward Lock), pp. 91-103.

LAMONT, W.A. (1970) 'The Uses and Abuses of Examinations', in M. Ballard (ed.) (1970), pp. 192-204.

PRICE, MARY (1968) 'History in Danger' in *History*, vol. 53, no. 179, pp. 342-7.

WAKE, R. (1970) 'History as a Separate Discipline: The Case' in *Teaching History*, vol. 1, no. 3, pp. 153-8.

Chapter 1

Why History?

Its study, the historian and the history teacher –what relationship?

If I may be permitted one heavily emphasised point, I must enter the reminder that history is a study of evidence, that there are no historical facts, only evidence. For our purposes, history is a narrative . . . constructed from evidence, that . . . we find acceptable. We are always concerned with the criteria of acceptability.

> R.A. Wake (1969) foreword in *History for Non-Specialists* (Harlow, Longmans, for the General Studies Association).

The problem then is not only concerned with syllabus and method of teaching, it is on a theoretical level about the viability of the subject and it comes from both educationists concerned with the psychology of learning and from historians concerned with the nature of their subject . . . . This mass attack cannot be answered upon the practical level alone. . . . We have to justify ourselves as history teachers not only to the children and students who sit in judgement upon us but to Professors Elton and Gittins.

> G. Jones (1970) 'Towards a Theory of History Teaching', in *History,* vol. 55, no. 183, p. 55.

This is baptism by total immersion but any study of "What history should we teach?' and 'How should we teach it?' logically depends upon the prior question 'Why do we teach it?' As the last chapter argued, this question has very rarely been carefully examined by writers on the teaching of history in schools. This is a real need because the issue is Janus-faced, where the teacher often finds himself almost trapped between his role as historian and educator. In the context of the comprehensive school, for example, how far can the study of the subject 'for its own sake' compete with the more 'useful' aims of social and political education?

The purpose of this first chapter is therefore to explore the issues deriving from the nature of history in order to help teachers decide for themselves the relationships and differences between the aims of the academic study of history and the needs for teaching history in schools. It examines these not only from the more familiar point of view of the historian, but also those of the philosopher of history and the epistemologist. This is essential because ultimately all these standpoints are used to justify the value, treatment and so place of history in the school curriculum. Thus this chapter introduces the problems of selection and method which follow.

HISTORY AS A DISCIPLINE: AGREEMENT ON PROCESS

What is History? The professional historian's response is usually
phrased in terms of process or activity — as illustrated by the number of
books entitled *Doing History, The Historian's Craft* or the *Practice of
History.* The element common to all of them is the concentration on
the *initial* process, examining what is particular in the historian's
approach to defining a problem, sifting the evidence, and evaluating it.
Amongst these books, that by Marc Bloch (1954) has always stood out,
but undoubtedly the best known contemporary rationale, and one that
would be generally accepted amongst historians, is that by Elton. The core
of his argument is that 'the purpose and ambition of the professional
historian is to understand a given problem from the inside'. Admitting
that this may well involve 'tedium, pettiness and pedantry', he argues
that this aim is unchallengeable because 'even at his worst' the historian
'cannot fail to add to learning, understanding and knowledge; he
contributes truth' (1967: 31). (Or, at least, he comes nearer to it!)

The claims of this analysis are reinforced by philosophers of knowledge. The concern of the epistemologists is whether history has a
unique place in the curriculum. Of contemporaries the best known is
Professor Hirst, and for him the justification of a subject is that it
should exhibit a particular mode of perception: 'a distinct way in
which our experience becomes structured around the use of accepted
public symbols' (1965: 128). From this definition he argues seven
distinct 'forms' of knowledge: history, the human sciences, mathematics,
the physical sciences, religion, literature and the fine arts and philosophy
This view is also supported and amplified by philosophers of history
such as Walsh (1951). One of their main concerns is to tease out the
meaning of the terms used in historical investigation. An example of this
is the term 'colligation', as developed by Walsh to describe the way in
which the historian needs to impose some grouping of events in order
to achieve explanation. To Walsh the aim of explanation is simply to
'illuminate' the facts so that the two basic criteria must be that the
grouping must be 'well founded as opposed to arbitrary' and 'tailored
to fit the facts' — a conclusion which again lends support to Elton's
functional definition.

THE VALUES OF HISTORY: DIFFERING OPINIONS

But 'What is the value of history?' At all levels history has always been
seen as being more than simply a discipline for investigating the past.
As Marwick argues, 'History is a social necessity'. It existed long before
its study became academic: history is to the community as memory is
to the individual (1970, ch. 1). Can 'historical truth' coexist with such
'social necessity'? Everyone knows who won Waterloo or, at least, he

thinks he does until he compares the various nationalist interpretations — as did Dance (1960)! If there is general agreement on the process of history, discussion of its cultural values or messages always provokes dissension. The time when Professor von Ranke was able to assert that 'we must work in two directions, the investigation of the effective factors in historical events and the understanding of their universal relationship' is long past.[1]

(1) *Historians' divisions over purpose*

Amongst professional historians, the controversy can be illustrated by comparing the philosophies of Professors Elton and Plumb. The former develops his arguments (above) to stigmatise most attempts at broad interpretation. He sees these as either 'evolutionary' — tending to see 'the hand of God in history', or 'present-minded' — deterministic in selecting 'the line of events and detail which leads to . . . their preconceived end' (1967: 47, 65). By contrast, Professor Plumb, though he admits that the restricted view is 'sound, sensible and cautious', argues that it 'still leaves unanswered the deeper question, the understanding of what? A human character, an event in time, the nature of an institution, of the reasons for belief? The progression rises. Dare it lift to the process of history itself?' (1969: 35). The immediate purpose of Elton's argument was, of course, to emphasise the dangers of false bias but what is really at issue is a wider question. It is that of the role of historian as communicator; is he writing solely for his fellow professional or for some wider public?

The obvious example of this controversy is the storm which greeted Toynbee's epic.[2] But perhaps a better illustration comes from the critical reception of the UNESCO *History of Mankind.* This work not only set out to be a-political but to present 'all subjects, however controversial, in such a way as to place them in their total context and to enhance understanding on all sides' — every section had to be approved by a committee of experts. Yet when it appeared it was attacked not only by the Marxist-Leninist historians but also 'traditional Western European liberals' and the Catholics, none of whose standpoints was satisfied. As Professor Aron summarised, 'in the last analysis the issue involves a difference as to what history should be . . . the authors have wished above all for it to be descriptive, neutral, objective, acceptable to everybody. Personally, I believe that it can only be problematic, interpretative, sociological, philosophical, unacceptable to some people' (Ware, 1966: 17, 20).[3] Put another way the purposes that motivate historians appear as a spectrum, ranging between the poles of Marxist economic determinism and Collingwood's 'idealism', the attempt to get inside the mind of the individual. If historians cannot agree on their purposes should history teachers? Today the widening aims of teaching history make this issue of vital importance because of the resulting assertion that many of these aims 'distort' the values of the subject.

(2) *Philosophers' divisions over explanation*

A similar contrast is to be found in the disagreements between philosophers of history on, for example, 'explanation'. A particularly interesting case is to set Professor Walsh's expansion of his understanding of 'colligation' (1967) against the theory of 'covering laws'. In this expansion Walsh argued that he had become more preoccupied with interpretation than with explanation alone: 'ideas of process, movement and development, should be taken as primary' (1967: 73). He was, therefore, concerned with the way in which an historian can single out the 'powerful thoughts, or spirit', inspiring a society during a period in the past. So he applauds Professor Briggs' choice of the 'Age of Improvement' to describe the period 1784-1867. However, the limitation on extending such grouping of interpretation must be stringently conceived if it is to meet the original criteria. By contrast the idea of a 'covering law' is that of being able to explain events or movements by reference to a set of common characteristics. Its origin lay in Popper's wish to argue the case for historical parallels to scientific explanations. Though greatly modified since it was originally conceived, the notion still attracts significant support from philosophers such as Gardiner, who base their case on the continuing need of the historians to use terms with general application, such as 'revolution'.[4]

(3) *Divisions on a philosophy for the curriculum*

Finally, it is important to emphasise the equally basic controversies that now also exist in epistemology. Since classical times rationality has been the *raison d'être* for epistemology. As Hirst puts it: 'the objectives of education are surely certain developments of the pupil that are achieved in learning and I suggest that these are all basically concerned with the development of a rational mind' (1969: 147). Recently, however, this rationalist framework has been challenged on the grounds of being both too restricting and even unreal.

An example of the first is the challenge raised by Professor Phenix in his *Realms of Meaning*. He is particularly concerned with the way in which fostering of values and attitudes and education of the emotions can be related to rational development. He has used the term 'realms of meaning' to introduce the dimensions of emotion, imagination and conscience, which he feels are restricted by a purely rationalist focus. For teachers this has now become a practical concern, both as a result of the encouragement of reports like Newsom and the development of more sophisticated objectives models for evaluating learning (see Chapter 7).

The second challenge is illustrated by the powerful critique of the conventional rationalist curriculum that has recently been advanced by sociologists, notably in M. Young's symposium (1971). The theme of their argument is that useful knowledge is in reality largely influenced by changing social attitudes, so that there can be no immutable or closed curriculum. Instead they feel that the curriculum must be 'open', 'reflecting the current values of the particular society'. Again the practical relevance and importance of this critique appears in the way in which the needs of the comprehensive school are challenging the conventional wisdoms of a subject curriculum designed primarily as a preparation for 'A' level and university entry.

HISTORY AND THE HISTORIAN

(1) *'Objective' and 'practical' history – the dilemma*

Do history teachers feel that the argument of the previous section has been moving away from their concerns? The aim has been to demonstrate that there can be no simple or single rationale for the value of history (and so for its place in the curriculum). Most important of all, has it not served to bring out that writing history has within it a constant and insoluble tension – which Oakeshott (1962) has so cleverly described as between the 'objective' and 'practical' pasts. The former reflects the historian's wish to create unbiased explanation, while the latter acknowledges the social pressures on him to interpret and communicate his findings to the society of which he forms a part.

The debate on the validity of the study of 'contemporary history' offers perhaps the best illustration of this tension because the millennial atmosphere of the twentieth century has given it real urgency. As Thomson put it: 'such is the nature of contemporary history that the demand for higher synthesis, for more coherent and comprehensive presentation of the long term trends of our times, will continue to grow. If it is not satisfied by competent professional historians it will be fobbed off with slipshod generalities or propagandist doctrines masquerading as historical truths.' (1967: 30). Critics, on the other hand, have made much play with three special difficulties in the study of this field: with the uneven qualities of the evidence; with the living historian's lack of detachment from 'personal interest and group loyalties'; and, above all, with his lack of hindsight – his judgement is bound to be so 'provisional' as not to be properly historical. Contemporary historians themselves acknowledge the special challenge of 'working on, or close to, the frontier of history', but argue strongly that their study, though more provisional because of the incompleteness of the evidence, is just as disciplined as that of other historians.[5] Thomson (1967) also adds that the increasingly rapid rate of change and speedier availability of evidence mean that this criticism is really relative.[6] The relevance and application of this issue become particularly apparent in the next chapter — because the fastest growing field in history teaching is undoubtedly that of twentieth-century syllabuses.

(2) *The teaching of history: theory into practice*

It is interesting to see how Oakeshott's view has recently been forcibly restated for teaching at the university: 'The mere establishment of the facts about the past is, in our view, a futile exercise for an historian, though appropriate for an antiquarian. . . . it deals with esoteric subjects and shows an increasing tendency towards jargon and quasi-scientific terminology. A "contemporary" approach, which we are advocating, involves the reconstruction of the parts of the past which have relevance for the historian who undertakes it, and contemporary significance for society as a whole.' (Connell-Smith & Lloyd, 1972:18). Teaching history, in other words, has to admit to the application of purpose.

TEACHING HISTORY IN SCHOOL

(1) *The traditional weaknesses*

Schooling is preparation and so history in school is always argued to be an introduction. Writers and teachers have generally agreed that this should aim to be an 'introduction' to historical thinking. As an aside, it must be admitted however that, until very recently, the practice of the traditional approach reversed and even perverted this aim. It reversed it by concentrating almost exclusively upon tertiary materials and compilations (rather than primary evidence) and perverted it by linking teaching to an examination system based upon memory recall: 'understanding consists of views received by the pupil at second or third hand from his teacher or the textbooks, and as conscientiously memorised as the names of the foreign ministers of the Great Powers' (Giles & Neal, 1973: 21). If the questions in certificate and degree examination papers appeared similar, yet notions of an introduction to the adult subject or to the work of the historian were ideal rather than actual — as the failure of Dr Happold's attempt to develop an 'historical training' showed.

In the last ten years, however, this practice has been questioned at all levels. For the average pupil the traditional approach has been roundly indicted — *vide* Mary Price. Even the apparently successful specialised education of the 'A' level elite has been criticised; Elton argues that for too many pupils the concentration upon interpretation is 'manifestly premature' because he feels that, rather than becoming extremely aware of the complexities involved in judgement, the pupil tends to gain a feeling of omniscience.[7]

(2) *The case for 'an introduction to historical thinking'*

The only writer who has developed a comprehensive analysis of the relationship between the nature of history and its teaching in the schools is W.H. Burston. His influence both as writer and teacher has been enormous because of the unique way in which his clear analysis of the philosophic principles of the subject has linked the thinking of the professional historian to that of the teacher. His argument is that for any introduction to historical thinking to succeed it must have 'sufficient penetration into the subject and its discipline' for the pupil to become accustomed to 'the characteristic mode of thought for the subject' (1971: 186). He sees this mode of thought as being based on understanding three notions: what is an historical fact, what constitutes historical explanation and what are the criteria for selection. To Burston all of these rest upon the special qualities of the first, these being a combination of the past, the human and the particular. Historical explanation has to be matched to these criteria and so it must be limited, as in colligation — Burston is very explicit about distinguishing such an explanation from that of the social sciences. Almost alone of contemporary writers on the teaching of history Burston can be said to define boundaries of legitimacy for the teacher to consider.

He is also very aware that teaching needs to take account of the pupil and the teacher as well as the subject — the famous and eternal triangle! He brings this out most clearly in his discussion of the crucial issue of selection, because it has to reflect the need to motivate through study in depth of the 'human and the particular' against the teacher's wish to communicate some perspective of change and a sense of time. On more recent developments, however, such as the 'project' method, the teaching of contemporary history and inter-disciplinary approaches, Burston's writing has tended to discuss their philosophic acceptability rather than to examine such approaches in practice (or how teachers are responding to them). As a result his work here needs to be supplemented by more specific analysis and comparisons. Also, his views emerge as perhaps more appropriate to the education of the examination candidate who is aiming at university entrance. His writing has not discussed in any detail the needs of the 'average' pupil and so the more immediate preoccupations of teachers in comprehensive or middle schools.

PROBLEMS OF IMPLEMENTATION

(1) *Simulating the activity of the historian*
How far can an 'introduction to historical thinking' simulate the
historical process? As his definition suggests, Burston is sceptical and
cautious. He points to the pupil's limited ability to handle evidence,
particularly his difficulty in coping with the problems of language and
context, and argues that these must demand rigorous selection and
skilful mediation by the teacher. He feels the same criticism can often
be levelled at project work, where the teacher's need to define the issue
and to select the evidence can falsify any genuine enquiry. Both these
objections are worthy of serious consideration, as there is no doubt
some exaggerated claims have been advanced. At the same time other
writers like John Fines or John West (Fines, 1969) feel that the use of
tangible and physical evidence can obviate Professor Burston's first
case and that his objection is only applicable where the evidence
requires sophisticated analysis and interpretation, as is often the case
with documents. To his second objection the same teachers would
reply that pupils are perfectly capable of conducting original enquiries
so long as they are limited in range or local in application, and Burston's
criticism really relates more to the earlier style of project which was
usually aimed at illuminating general issues in national history.

In sum, these history writers of the new school are urging the teacher
to specify particular objectives rather than be content with generalised
statements such as 'an introduction to historical thinking'. They feel
that this aim needs to be developed in particular contexts, against
knowledge of the individual pupil's ability to master language, time
concepts and organising ideas. In other words, in order to understand
and establish the ways in which pupils can become legitimately involved
in the historical process one needs to relate the philosophy of the
subject to the results of educational research — as described in the third
chapter.

(2) *Selection and legitimacy*
Selection is undoubtedly the most controversial aspect of history
teaching because it can bring the teacher's historical values into direct
conflict with his role as an educator. The premium placed on content
aims, shown in any survey of history teaching, indicates the teacher's
inescapable commitment to communication, a commitment which
brings out the essential difference between his role and that of the
professional historian. The key to these differences lies in application.
As described earlier, the nature of the professional's study normally
leads him to concentrate upon a single 'aspect' of history and to apply
strict limitations when grouping events or linking periods. Does not the

nature of a school history syllabus, however, raise problems of range and explanation in a way rarely encountered by the professional historian?

As an example of the first, consider 'world history' – one of the fastest-growing sectors in history teaching in the last decade – and the difficulties of defining any syllabus for this in terms of chronology and content. If the immediate problems of selecting areas and periods appear daunting, the need to set these within some 'legitimate' historical framework of interpretation is even more exacting. As the criticisms of the UNESCO attempt brought out, professional historians who have attempted this task have never succeeded in satisfying all their colleagues – and there is still no university in this country which offers a degree in world history! Secondly, there is the further need within every syllabus to articulate the general framework in a way which makes intelligible social, economic, political and cultural perspectives, while matching these to study of the 'human and particular'. Here the principles of the debate on 'explanation' become directly relevant for the teacher because of the way in which case-studies and concept-frameworks are being increasingly used to achieve this, particularly in twentieth-century and world history syllabuses. Here again the professional historian's concentration upon his particular case means that he does not have to meet the problem in this way. This was brought out at the inter-disciplinary conferences on 'fascism' at Reading, where the general political or economic models proposed by the social scientists never satisfied the historians' 'particular' cases.[8]

So, even more acutely than in interpreting 'process', the applied needs of syllabus-making force the teacher to decide how to reconcile his historical training with his role as educator. Again, however, the only way in which he can properly assess the real implications of such general considerations is by analysing them in terms of the specific characters of different approaches. This is the concern of the next chapter.

NOTES

1. Quoted in Stern (1956), p. 62.
2. For those interested in this debate Toynbee's final volume *Reconsiderations,* in which he replies to his critics, is endlessly fascinating and illuminating.
3. See Carolyn Ware (ed.) (1966), *The History of Mankind: Cultural and Scientific Development,* vol. 6, parts 1 and 2 (London, Allen & Unwin).
4. This whole debate has been well summarised in Perry's article in Burston and Thompson (1967).
5. See in particular Watts' account of the developing perspective on the

Suez Crisis in Ballard (1970).
6. To illustrate this, it can be argued that views of Alexander the Great have seen just as much reinterpretation during the last forty years as studies of Hitler since Bullock.
7. In Ballard (1970), p. 224.
8. Seʳ S. Woolf (ed.) (1968) *European Fascism* (London, Weidenfeld), and (1969) *The Nature of Fascism* (London, Weidenfeld).

BIBLIOGRAPHY

The study of history and its place in the curriculum.

BALLARD, M. (ed.) (1970) *New Movements in the Study and Teaching of History* (London, Temple Smith).

BARRACLOUGH, G. (1964) *History in a Changing World* (Oxford, Blackwell).

___ (1967) *History and the Common Man* (London, Historical Association).

BERNBAUM, G. (1967-8) 'Sociology and Contemporary History' in *Educational Review,* vol. 20, pp. 191-203.

BLOCH, M. (1954) *The Historians' Craft* (Manchester U.P.)

BURSTON, W.H. and THOMPSON, D. (1967) *Studies in the Nature and Teaching of History* (London, Routledge).

CARR, E.H. (1964) *What is History?* (Harmondsworth, Penguin).

COMMAGER, H.S. (1965) *The Nature and the Study of History* (New York, Merrill).

CONNELL-SMITH, G. and LLOYD, A.H. (1972) *The Relevance of History* (London, Heinemann).

DANCE, E.H. (1960) *History the Betrayer* (London, Hutchinson).

ELTON, G.R. (1967) *The Practice of History* (London, Fontana).

FINBERG, H. (1962) *Approaches to History* (London, Routledge).

HEXTER, J.H. (1971) *Doing History* (London, Allen & Unwin).

HIRST, P.H. (1965) 'Liberal Education and the Nature of Knowledge' in R. Archambault (ed.) *Philosophical Analysis and Education* (London, Routledge) pp. 113-40.

___ (1969) 'The Logic of the Curriculum', in *Journal of Curriculum Studies,* vol. 1, no. 2, pp. 142-58.

HISTORICAL ASSOCIATION (1969) *The Place and Purpose of History* (London).

HOLLOWAY, S.W.F. (1967) 'History and Sociology: What History Is and What It Ought To Be', in Burston and Thompson (1967) pp. 1-25.

KITSON-CLARK, G. (1967) The Critical Historian (London, Heinemann).

MARWICK, A. (1970) *The Nature of History* (London, Macmillan).

___ (1970-1) *What History Is and Why Is It Important?; The Writing of History; Common Pitfalls in Historical Writing,* Units 5, 7, 8 of Open University Humanities Foundation Course.

OAKESHOTT, M. (1962) 'The Activity of Being a Historian', in *Rationalism in Politics* (London, Methuen) pp. 137-67.

PERRY, L.R. (1967) 'The Covering Law Theory of Historical Explanation', in Burston and Thompson (1967) pp. 27-48.

PHENIX, P.(1964) *Realms of Meaning* (New York, McGraw-Hill).

PLUMB, J.H. (1969) *The Death of the Past* (Harmondsworth, Penguin).

ROGERS, P. (1972) 'History', in K. Dixon, *Philosophy of Knowledge and the Curriculum* (Oxford, Pergamon), pp. 75-134.

STERN, F. (1956) *The Varieties of History from Voltaire to the Present* (New York, Meridian).

THOMSON, D. (1967) 'The Writing of Contemporary History' in *Journal of Contemporary History,* vol. 2, no. 1, pp. 25-34.

___(1969) *The Aims of History* (London, Thames & Hudson).

WALSH, W. (1951) *Introduction to the Philosophy of History* (London, Hutchinson).

___(1967) 'Colligatory Concepts in History', in Burston and Thompson (1967), pp. 65-83.

WATT, D.C. (1970) '20th Century History', in M. Ballard (ed.) (1970) pp. 62-75.

WHITFIELD, R. (ed.) (1971) *Disciplines of the Curriculum* (New York, McGraw-Hill).

YOUNG, M. (ed.) (1971) *Knowledge and Control* (New York, Collier-Macmillan).

Teaching History

BOOTH, M. (1969) *History Betrayed* (Harlow, Longmans).

BURSTON, W.H. (1971 rev. edn) *Principles of History Teaching* (London, Methuen). See also articles in Burston and Thompson (1967) and Burston and Green (ed.) (1972) *Handbook for History Teachers* (London, Methuen).

COLLISTER, P. (1972) 'History Teaching Today', in *Trends in Education,* no. 27, pp. 2-5.

ELTON, G.R. (1970) 'What Sort of History Should We Teach?', in Ballard (1970), pp. 221-30.

FINES, J. (1969) 'The Teaching of Pre-History' in J. Fines (ed.) *History: Blond's Teachers' Handbooks* (London, Blond), pp. 1-19.

___(1970) *The History Teacher and Other Disciplines* (London, Historical Association).

GILES, Phyllis (1973) 'History in the Secondary School: A Survey', in *Journal of Curriculum Studies,* vol. 5, pp. 133-44.

GILES, Phyllis and NEAL, G. (1973) 'History Teaching Analysed', in *Trends in Education,* no. 32, pp. 16-25.

HENDERSON, J.L. (ed.) (1966) *Since 1945, Aspects of Contemporary World History* (London, Methuen).

___(1968) *Education for World Understanding* (Oxford, Pergamon).

JOHNSON, H. (1940, rev. edn) *The Teaching of History in Elementary and Secondary Schools* (London, Macmillan).

KRUG, M.M. (1967) *History and the Social Sciences: New Approaches to the Teaching of Social Studies* (Trans-Atlantic Book Service, Blaisdell).

ROGERS, A. (1961-2) 'Why Teach History? The Answer of Fifty Years', in *Educational Review,* vol. 14, no. 1 (1961), pp. 10-20 and no. 2 (1962), pp. 152-62.

WEST, J. (1969) 'The Middle Ages', in J. Fines (ed.) *History: Blond's Teachers' Handbooks* (London, Blond), pp. 36-50.

Chapter 2

What History Should We Teach?

Subject values and teaching aims–a tension?

Many of the syllabuses seen in the course of the survey were
undergoing a process of reappraisal and refashioning. It appeared,
however, that the principal matter of concern was choice of content
. . . Freshly conceived and thought out aims, stated in broad terms
but closely geared to a comprehensive consideration of methods and
teaching resources, were scarcely to be found in a single syllabus.
One cause for this is doubtless a healthy reluctance to prefix the
syllabus with a string of platitudes to which no more than lip
service need be paid. At the present time, however, it seems
imperative not only to rethink aims and objectives appropriate to
the changing concept of the subject, but also to restate them.

> Phyllis Giles (1973) 'History in the Secondary School: A Survey',
> in *Journal of Curriculum Studies*, vol. 5, p. 135.

The kind of bias that ought to be discussed more seriously is the
distortion which underlies the very structure of the syllabus. The
history teacher, more than any other, is overwhelmed by the sheer
immensity of potential teaching material. . . . In ruthlessly selecting
a minute proportion of this vast stock he is carrying a burden of
which he is rarely fully aware. . . . Because it is impossible to study
the whole of world history the overt act of selection is itself an act
of distortion.

> D. Heater (1964) 'What History Should We Teach?', in
> *Education for Teaching,* no. 65, p. 46.

INTRODUCTION: THE IMPORTANCE OF CONTENT

This chapter is about content: 'what history do we teach?' The
immediate impression from the syllabuses in any cross-section of
schools today must be of their variety, almost a kaleidoscope in range
and time. Within these syllabuses the obvious contrast is one of
approach, between limited topics which make strong use of historical
evidence and outline surveys which feature breadth and continuity.
This contrast, however, oversimplifies; for it is so often cut across both
by the range of the syllabuses and the underlying emphases within
them. In range this becomes very apparent when the conventional
national focus is raised to the global setting necessary for the twentieth
century, or subordinated to that of comparing civilisations: in emphasis
when the traditional mainstream of constitutional development and

international relations is either narrowed to bring out the human effects of technological advance or social change, or again broadened in an attempt to develop some comparison between cultures. Does not this prompt the further question: 'what history should we teach'? This is, of course, much more difficult. On the one hand it begs some rationale for the study of the subject, such as that offered by Burston. On the other hand, does it not demand a justification for the choice of specific content; in effect some answer to that third and most difficult of Roy Wake's questions – 'What difference will it make to us if we did not possess it [i.e. information about the past] ?'

CONTEMPORARY CONTEXT

(1) *Developments*

So there are two ways of viewing this question. The first is through the doing – practical developments. The obvious problem of the content of history is its immensity: 'the whole recorded experience of man in time'. History cannot avoid being an information subject but a main problem has always been 'the evident fear that the body of fact may be over-estimated, or badly chosen, or misused'.[1] The vital need is to make this 'relevant', though the generalised nagging of reports and official pamphlets has worked this term almost to death. From this standpoint the experience of the last ten years appears comforting. There have been significant developments in trying to bring the subject within the interests and grasp of the pupils – to encourage motivation. In presentation, the traditional monolithic narrative of the 'island' story has been dramatically modified into vivid but still 'important' studies of periods or topics. Parallel with this has been the growth of 'evidential studies', which·seek to develop the pupil's human curiosity towards the beginning of an understanding of how we know about the past – the historian's activity and its discipline. Lastly, the millennial atmosphere of the twentieth century and its growing social conscience and consciousness has influenced teachers to extend the island story much further into the twentieth century and towards the present – which accords well with the pressing social aims of comprehensive schooling.

To 'transmit a sense of heritage' has always been the history teacher's concern – the subject has been the traditional vehicle for social and political education. This is clearly reflected in the traditional syllabus. The theme here was constitutional and imperial – the evolution of democracy at home and the building of an empire overseas. It so obviously emphasises its late nineteenth-century origin, the era of Actonian certainty, which looked to history teaching to popularise what would then have appeared as the unique qualities of the British –

stability at home and success abroad. Any survey of history teaching today not only reflects the same kind of concern for content but shows a noticeable widening of such concerns. For example, in a local Cambridgeshire survey in 1970, 'The Teaching of History to the 11-14 age group', four of the eight sets of 'objectives' referred to content: 'to impart knowledge — for example, to introduce pupils to the famous eras of British and world history; to give a sense of time and of the development of ideas and institutions; to show how the past explains the present; to develop a civic and social purpose and lead to a greater measure of international understanding; to develop an understanding of heritage'.[2]

(2) *Problems of over-generalisation*

Listing these trends and 'objectives' appears comforting, both to those teachers who feel their subject to be under attack and to the others who feel they want to experiment. But is this not all too generalised? As the 1973 HMI survey pointed out, very few schools develop any such rationale for their syllabuses.[3] More important, any more detailed analysis of either the trends or the 'objectives' only tends to raise more questions. The last chapter emphasised how history teaching has to 'apply' the values of history. How far can an adolescent seriously attempt to simulate the sophisticated craft of the adult professional historian? More important here, do not the 'objectives', in supporting the demand for 'topical relevance', use or even distort the subject? As Derek Heater highlights, this is the issue that has caused the greater controversy. Following the argument of the previous chapter, the need is for some fundamental justification to try and identify 'criteria' for selection — criteria which ensure a place for the values of history alongside the wider aims of history teaching.

Do not the teachers' 'objectives' seem to pose two immediate questions? First, the word itself surely implies something which can be seen to be achieved — or preferably measured. How far do the four 'objectives' cited meet this definition? Certainly they are attractive but are they not too generalised to infer how they should be translated into syllabuses — surely they are ideals or goals and might better be termed aims? So is not the first need to break through this vagueness towards being more specific? Again, the four aims are surely too diverse to conceive of their being reconciled within any one 'ideal syllabus' — and the British tradition would surely not wish this to happen. So the second important question is whether such diverse aims can respect common criteria of principle.

CRITERIA FOR SELECTION: A RATIONALE

Once again the only thorough analysis of principles in syllabus-making in terms of the value of history has been that by Burston.[4] He isolated two criteria: that a syllabus should possess a clearly defined aim and that it should suit the abilities of the pupils for whom it is designed. As he says, the concern of the latter is primarily with the capabilities of the pupil — the psychological determinants which are the subject of the next chapter. However, when 'motivation' is given central importance, suitability has an obvious influence on the selection of content — for example in Jeffreys' advocacy of 'the lines of development' approach for younger pupils (1939). The focus of this chapter, however, must be upon the first criterion, that of defining an aim. As the Cambridge-shire survey emphasises, the contrast in objectives naturally makes this the area of greater controversy.

By aim Burston means the 'concept' of history implicit in any syllabus and argues that any such concept must be developed from two considerations: the particular selection of events and the theory of interpretation which links them and so gives coherence and *purpose* to the syllabus. He goes on that the criterion for selecting events is obviously that of their 'importance', but stresses that this is not as simple a definition as it might appear. It involves not only judgements of the impact of events, such as Hampden's stand over ship-money, but, through the hindsight exercised by the historian, the identification of less obvious but nonetheless significant trends, such as the growing humanitarianism in the seventeenth century argued by Trevelyan. He shows that the normal criterion applied in either case will be that of 'what affects most people' but emphasises that this choice is based on the teacher taking a value position — a point that is often overlooked. The corollary is fundamental: the rejection of history as a body of 'received knowledge' even for teaching. Secondly, Burston stresses how the linking framework must be a *theory* of interpretation. Far from being objective this may ultimately reflect a personal viewpoint though it is more likely to follow some accepted tradition or conviction. If the conventional syllabus is taken as an example, it is obvious that importance has mainly been determined by the Western European liberal tradition.

He concludes, therefore, that the properly constructed syllabus should offer a balance of studies of the human and particular 'without which the imaginative appeal of history is lost', within a linking frame-work of interpretation — a matrix of *horizontal* and *vertical* perspectives. Lastly he reminds us that the primary aim of the historian is to enter into the past and 'to understand its people better than they understood themselves'. Consequently he argues that the need for an interpretive frame must never dominate selection as, for example, using the lessons of the past in order to make some prediction for present actions or future development.

The value of Burston's analysis is to suggest a method for making useful comparisons across syllabuses, by examining the ways in which the criteria of importance and suitability inform approaches. This is not to say that there will be a single 'right' or 'ideal' approach for, as the previous chapter brought out, there is no simple or single rationale for the study of history itself. What we are arguing is that, by doing this, we might be able to achieve greater clarity on the principles of what we are about in history teaching.

THE CONVENTIONAL SYLLABUS AND ITS MODIFICATION

(1) *Criticism of the traditional approach*

The last decade has seen violent and often vicious criticisms of history teaching, not only that voiced by pupils — the vituperative, almost unprintable, example in Willmot, but also from teachers, as in the Cambridgeshire survey. What is the substance of these? First and foremost is the accusation of 'dullness' — of a history which still appears today little more than the endless catechism of dates, facts and kings so acidly parodied by Sellars and Yeatman forty years ago. The main cause of such apparent insistence on rigid order and continuity is generally seen to be the influence of chronology. As Giles and Neal note, there has been a violent backlash against this. But they add, 'it has yet to be demonstrated that a historical sense can be acquired without [it]' (1973: 18). How important is it to develop a time-sense through the syllabus structure? Do not most pupils lack a developed sense of time before sixteen (so that both the range of the traditional syllabus and the implicit concepts like change/continuity are really too difficult for most of them to grasp)?[5] Also, if this approach is to communicate a sense of the 'continuous past', of how 'heritage' or the present grew up, it also surely means that it has to be covered at the summary level of generality that again Sellars and Yeatman parodied so well. The second criticism follows from this. It is that of the impersonality of the approach, usually resulting from a focus on the growth of the nation state. History should be concerned with the 'actuality' of human affairs, but does not this perspective tend to lead teachers to over-emphasise political and economic development, movements which are difficult to represent except at a level of abstract generalisation? This reinforces the dullness of the approach for pupils who find it irrelevant to the direct or even imaginative experience which they can enjoy and understand.

(2) *Motivation and the 'patch' approach*
How far are these criticisms any longer valid? As the introduction argues, 'dullness' has been attacked from three directions during the last ten years. Surely any teacher designing a syllabus today accepts the value of the patch approach. The first, and now famous, advocacy was that by Peter Carpenter in his *Era Approach.* (see Chart 1).

Chart 1 A PATCH SYLLABUS FOR BRITISH HISTORY

B.C.	The Stone Age
	Egypt under the Pharaohs
900	
800	
700	
600	
500	Fifth-Century Athens
400	
300	Rome and Carthage
200	
100	

YEAR 1

100	
	Roman Britain
200	
300	
400	
500	

600	
700	
800	The Time of King Alfred
900	
1000	The Coming of the Normans
1100	
1200	The Near and Far East
1300	The World of Chaucer
1400	
1500	The Renaissance Era
	The Days of Queen Elizabeth I
1600	
	The Restoration Period

YEAR 2

1700	The Age of Revolutions: (I) Britain (II) Europe (III) Overseas
1800	
	Mid-Victorian Times America during the Civil War
1900	The British Empire at its Height

YEAR 3

	The Edwardian Scene The Struggle for Power The Thirties
A.D.	The Second World War The Nuclear Age Britain in the
	Nuclear Age

YEAR 4

Source: P. Carpenter (1964) *The Era Approach* (Cambridge University Press), pp. 90-1.

He argued that it was possible to show history as a living past by breaking up the monolithic narrative into 'eras' within which there would be a cross-sectional analysis embracing 'social customs, religious issues, the arts' alongside the concern for political development. His examples of 'The Age of Chaucer' or 'The Elizabethan Age' are now so well known that they do not need to be further elaborated. Carpenter also advocated that, as far as possible, the enquiry should be 'handed over . . . to the pupils themselves' (1964: 37). In these ways he shows himself as a pioneer, not only in modifying the traditional approach, but also in leading the general trend towards enquiry-based education.

Margaret Bryant has added further dimensions to this rationale in her article 'General and Aspect History' (1972), which discusses developing a patch on the seventeenth century (see Chart 2).

Chart 2 THE DEVELOPMENT OF A PATCH
English history in the seventeenth century

---

1. Outline of period, 1603–88.
2. 'The Queen is dead, long live the King !' – England in 1603.
3. Englishmen abroad in the early seventeenth century – Virginia, East India and Muscovy Companies.
4. Shakespeare's *Tempest* – the Jacobean imagination.
5. The village and the parish in the early seventeenth century.
6. The country gentry in the early seventeenth century.
7. Artists and the Stuart Court – Inigo Jones, Rubens and Van Dyck.
8. The Thirty Years' War.
9.
10. Political events in England, 1603–42, and the Civil War.
11. Dutch life and art in the seventeenth century.
12. Two contrasting 'studies in tyranny' – Louis XIV and Oliver Cromwell.
13. A tour of England at the time of the Restoration.
14. Establishment, non-conformity, toleration – John Bunyan.
15. Samuel Pepys, London and the Navy.
16. Science in the seventeenth century – an intellectual revolution related to its age.
17. Milton and *Paradise Lost* – to explore and enjoy the Baroque imagination.
18. Village and town, parish and diocese.
19. Political events in the reign of Charles II – the Popish Plot.
20. Business and commercial life of London in later seventeenth century.
21. A survey of Baltic affairs in the later seventeenth century.
22. Macaulay's History of England and the Revolution of 1688.

Source: Margaret E. Bryant (1972) General and Aspect History, in W.H. Burston and C.W. Green (eds), *Handbook for History Teachers* (London, Methuen), p. 101.

First, she argues more directly for the inclusion and use of source material. For example, she describes how an understanding of the role of 'the country gentry in the seventeenth century' can be sharpened by drawing upon diaries, biographies and even estate records. Similarly she argues that a study of, for example, 'artists and the Stuart Court' can make more than decorative use of, for example, the paintings of Van Dyck. Her second assertion is even more important. She develops Carpenter's 'cross-sectional' thesis to argue the central importance of social history in the patch, following Perkins' view that 'political and economic historians are aware of the social framework underpinning the economic and political system at every point'. So, her study of the country gentry is aimed not only to show the way of life in the 'Great House' but to lead on to some understanding of the concerns and so involvement of the 'country party' in constitutional affairs. In the same way the cultural study of the Court is aimed at developing an understanding of its character: 'the obstinacy and insecurity of the Cavaliers and their problems' (1972: 103, 110). The major issue in the patch is still the conventional one of the conflict between King and Parliament, but Margaret Bryant feels that by using this approach, a basic understanding will be built up in a way that will make the conflict seem meaningful to the pupils – and hopefully it will be better remembered!

The third way in which history teachers have sought to encourage motivation amongst their pupils is by involving them in actively investigating the past. A major stimulus here has been the accelerating interest amongst historians in studying both the locality and novel 'aspect' histories, such as oral tradition and demography. The obvious attraction of such approaches for teaching is their immediacy, and their ability to involve the pupil in investigating evidence. If local history was originally introduced into schools mainly in order to illustrate national issues, writers like Robert Douch have argued that such studies 'should become a jumping off base for the unknown or a focus and yardstick for comparison and contrast . . . local, national and world studies should be essentially complementary' (1972: 86). A parallel growth area has been that of family history. While its general appeal is the same as that for local study, the difference is that it lays particular emphasis upon the use of oral evidence and the experience of the individual. Using the similarities and contrasts within the experiences of the families of a group of pupils, the teacher can help the pupils to re-create a 'meaningful' past – where the impact of national events is seen through the eyes of the individual.

For the upper school such a justification can acquire a further dimension. John Fines (1970: 16) cites the example of E.P. Thompson as a historian who has accepted all the tools that the other disciplines present him: 'This brilliant study would repay the close attention of every teacher interested in expanding his armour in a constructive, sensible and profoundly educational way.'[6] This opinion is echoed in Derek Turner's introduction to his pamphlet *Historical Demography in Schools:* 'It has a strong mathematical emphasis, it involves pupils in finding out for themselves and trying to work out for themselves the significance of what they have discovered; it links history to other school subjects such as geography and economics, and provides a lead-in to social science topics. . . . It is to be hoped that more and more teachers will come to appreciate the nature of the subject and realise its value in broadening and deepening the education of their pupils.' (1971: 7).

The obvious limitation for all these evidential approaches is their restricted coverage. So, to follow Burston's argument, they can help to promote the 'horizontal' perspective, but will still need to be set within some 'vertical' perspective of interpretation.

The general impact of these three styles of modifying and revaluing traditional presentation is surely no longer disputed. There are, however, two points worth restating. The first is the way in which evidential approaches have been leading teachers to draw upon a much wider range of evidence than the documentary for their teaching. As the next chapter shows, some would claim to be able to use such an approach successfully even in the junior school. At the same time it is worth re-emphasising how the use of the original evidence is becoming much more widespread at sixth form level (though teaching here has always been based upon the comparison of interpretation). The second point is more important − the revaluing of 'aspect' history in developing explanation.

Here Margaret Bryant's argument for social history is only the most obvious case. Because of its focus upon people and particular situations, social history has long been regarded as well suited to the interests and abilities of children in upper junior and lower secondary schools. If this attitude has been rather condescending, shown by its application to the teaching of topics such as 'homes' or 'clothes', Miss Bryant's argument has clearly demonstrated the real importance of such studies. They can affect the sixth former as much as the 12-year-old − it is worth noting how 'A' level teachers in the recent Schools Council survey wanted to develop many more such 'aspect' approaches.[7]

(3) *The aim of 'heritage' and its problems*
If the traditional approach has mainly been attacked on grounds of presentation, it is also claimed to be of 'little apparent relevance'. Contained in the report by the Cambridgeshire teachers were assertions by vocal minorities that the conventional approach to transmitting

heritage was far too limited both in its theme and its range. None of the modifications discussed so far have raised this question, as the illustration from Margaret Bryant shows. However, in syllabus making, it should surely be primary. Perhaps what is being brought out is how much the development and acceptance of the patch approach in national history has really depended upon an overall hierarchy of agreements on the purpose of narrating it — that is on the meaning of heritage. This agreement has depended upon the teachers' familiarity with the overall narrative, a familiarity secured by its having formed the core of their own historical education and which is in turn perpetuated by the continuing dominance of such courses in university teaching — so the hierarchy. One might debate or challenge the nature of the 'Tudor Revolution in Government' but no one would question the central importance of the Tudors! Nevertheless, might it not be claimed that it is this conventional agreement that tends to result in a focus upon relatively sophisticated academic controversies that make the past seem more remote to many pupils and their teachers — and so leads them to feel that the content of the syllabus is lacking in 'relevance' and that it would be more valuable to concentrate on 'explaining the present'?

(4) *Twentieth-century history and the extension of 'heritage'*

The immediate answer to this discontent has been to press for 'topical relevance' and to express this through extending the syllabus well into the twentieth century. The result is a crisis. It is partly caused by the quickening pace of change but it is much more acutely the result of the new dimensions of scale: the explanation of world wars, of continuing 'brinkmanship', of a 'Third World', of regional associations and international organisations — all make a world framework essential. Can English history any longer afford to stop at the Channel, or even the 'continong' known to Mr Punch? Again, particularly after 1945, is not a British standpoint of peripheral importance in many major issues and controversies — such as the Cuban missile crisis or the struggle against social injustice in 'black' Africa or America? The other problem that is raised in acute form is that issues here are obviously complex and also just as remote to the experience of most pupils.

Here none of the three modifying presentations seems entirely satisfactory. Peter Carpenter's era approach allotted one year's study out of four to the twentieth century, a total of eight out of his twenty-four six-week units. Yet, considering his suggested treatments at the end of his book, even this allocation seems insufficient. The word 'survey' reappears, recalling the possibility of the kinds of lecture teaching and summary generalisation that his approach was surely trying to avoid. Margaret Bryant, in her series *World Outlook 1900-1965*, has shown how such large issues can be broken down. But unless teachers formulate some limiting theory of interpretation, any attempt at complete coverage will involve a basic set of seventeen patches — which would demand an even more dramatic recasting of the syllabus! Again, if evidential approaches seem to offer some alternative — as in the way 'family history' enables pupils to approach subjects like the Second World War in a meaningful fashion (see Chart 3) — such 'aspect' approaches can be only a partial answer because of their obvious limitations in range.

TWENTIETH CENTURY HISTORY AND NEW APPROACHES

(1) *Understanding the present*

Is it possible to reconcile conventional 'heritage' with 'explaining the present'? Does not 'the very breadth compel a reconsideration of the approach' (DES, 1967: 4) — and so of the meaning of importance? (At the same time one must not forget that often the teacher is also being pressed to develop 'a sense of civic and social purpose' and to promote some measure of 'international understanding'.) So, in order to come to terms with such aims and to try to teach them in a way that pupils will find both attractive and intelligible, twentieth century history has stimulated basic reconsiderations of the conventional approach. This is a challenge to the boundaries of 'legitimacy' of the same order as that of the validity of contemporary history found amongst professional historians.

(2) *The thematic approach*

The first of the novel, or 'divergent', approaches has been to argue for selection by problem rather than by period. The suitability of this for twentieth-century history has already been pointed out by historians. Thomson, for example, argues that 'World relationships throw into relief general themes for historical study that are not the same as those projected by national, or even continental history. World population and food supply, the comparative study of institutions and social systems, racial relations, contrasts of culture and intellectual approach' (1969: 92). Further, the way in which such themes can be linked together to provide an overall explanation has been clearly developed by Barraclough: 'a skeleton or framework within which political action takes place' (1967: 16).

The advantages of this approach are immediately obvious. First, issues like nationalism can be argued not only to have basic importance in interpreting the present century but also as having 'topical' appeal — which happily coincides with the growing demands for social education. Next the theme gives a single frame of reference by comparison with

EVIDENCE

Motivation: to arouse the pupil's interest through personal involvement and the unearthing of first-hand evidence.

IDEAS

Aim: to develop the pupil's understanding of the impact of war upon society, using the example of World War 2.

TOPIC SETTING

Aim: introduces the need to evaluate particular experience against a wider background. To develop awareness of the diversity of historical resources. Skill: referencing, abstracting from and editing 1) Text and topic books 2) Contemporary sources, e.g. newspapers, photos etc., 3) Personalised evidence, e.g. biographies etc. 4) Artefacts: wartime and miscellania

---

STAGE 1: Individual Inquiry

STARTERS

Skill: collection and organisation of original source material.
Activity: interviewing parents and relatives using questionnaires and tape recorders. Range of experiences revealed by interviews included: merchant seamen, POW captured at Dunkirk, 8th Army infantryman, aircraft worker, sergeant fighter pilot, evacuee.

STAGE 2: Group Inquiry

Motivation: to sustain the pupil's interest in the project through the imaginative reconstruction of historical events.
Skills: authentification developed by group tasks, which placed individual experiences in the perspective of relevant key episodes and situations.
Activity: emphasis on role playing and drama, involving personal judgements. Presentation of results of group projects.

A1 The Blitz
Simulation: Fighter Command v. the Luftwaffe – a raid (jackdaw). Reconstruction: the experience of civilians and Home Defence during the same raid.

A2 The Mohne Dam
Research: developments in bombing capability during World War 2. Playlet: final rehearsal for the raid to demonstrate combatant involvement.

B1 Dunkirk
Activity: map showing stages of BEF's campaign up to time of evacuation. Reconstruction: the experience of a 'little boat's' crew involved in evacuation.

B2 El Alamein
Activity: sand table reconstruction of battle to demonstrate underlying strategy. Reconstruction: Private soldier's diary of the battle.

D1 Evacuation
Simulation: the problems of evacuating an area of London. Reconstruction: the experience of a London evacuee sent to the country (poems, short stories etc.).

D2 Working in an aircraft factory
Simulation: reconstruction of a 'worker's playtime' programme for the factory. Activity: collecting interviews with other women ex-workers (e.g. landgirls, ATS etc.).

C1 U boat campaign
Simulation: the Battle for the North Atlantic. Reconstruction: log of U boat commander's cruise.

C2 D Day landings
Research: the logistics and problems facing combined operations landings. The example of Mulberry. Reconstruction: slide-tape sequence illustrating individual experiences during D Day.

STAGE 3: Class Synthesis

Aim: to show the pupil how the historian uses particular evidence to inform his discussion of broader ideas. Using the evidence supplied by the group projects, to develop the pupil's understanding of aspects of the impact of war upon society. Skills: selection, presentation and communication of relevant conclusions from earlier individual and group work.

A1 & 2: Used as introductions to the theme 'Technology and Industry in Modern Warfare'. Cross-referred to C2 & D2.
B1 & 2: Used as introductions to 'Strategy' through examining two possible turning points in the war.
C1 & 2: Used as introduction to 'The Individual in War: the Combatant'. Cross referred to B2.
D1 & 2: Used as introduction to "The Individual in War: the Civilian" as part of the theme 'Total War'. Cross referred to A1 and B1.

Source: L. Taylor (1971)

the difficulties of global periodisation or balancing the relative importance of events on opposite sides of the world. This is also helpful when a purely British standpoint might appear peripheral in an issue of world importance, such as political freedom. Also, against arguments of simply being fashionable, the theme can advance a tradition of respectability — dating back to Jeffreys' advocacy of 'lines of development' and the claim for a 'developmental perspective'. The advantage over the chronological is that themes can be analysed through a limited number of 'case studies' and so allow the development of enquiry in depth — James Henderson's *World Questions: A Study Guide* shows how such issues can be handled intelligibly and attractively even for younger secondary pupils.

Facing this choice a teacher may well tend to be swept off his feet! If so, he ought to consider how far such an approach is acceptable to him as an historian. First, the choice as to which issues are significant is almost always based upon their importance for the present: 'making clear the structural framework of the world today'. Second, there is no consensus on the selection of themes. Compare, for example, the issues chosen by the historian Barraclough, with those of the Humanities Curriculum Project for social education, and those of the 'internationalist' reflected in James Henderson's selection (see Chart 4). Not only does each selection differ in its aim but, despite overlaps in choice, the basic differences in purpose always tend to stand out. For example, nationalism as it is usually treated appears essentially concerned with developing understanding of the nation as a political entity, while the 'Third World' is normally set within a frame of economic contrasts, and 'race relations' within a frame of human rights. Finally, since the purpose of the theme is to give greater coherence to selection (if it is not to result in an 'atomistic' approach), an important emphasis in teaching will usually be the identification of common or contrasting features from the illustrative case studies — which might detract from the historian's emphasis on the human context.

(3) *The approach of the social sciences*
The second novel organising framework that has been rapidly growing in popularity is that taken from the social sciences proper. The attraction of this approach also derives from the assumption that the important purpose is to understand the present — the direct purpose of the social sciences. (A distinction must be made here between the 'analytic' disciplines, which are usually those that the historian draws upon, and the 'prescriptive'.) The second claim of these disciplines is that their concepts have been developed to analyse structure and function, so they not only offer a clear framework for explanation but can also be used comparatively because they are, of their nature,

Chart 4 THE SELECTION OF THEMES

Barraclough

Industrialisation and imperialism
Population: the dwarfing of Europe
International relations: from the European balance of power to the age
  of world politics
Political organisation: individualism and mass democracy
The Third World: revolt against the West — African and Asian reaction
The ideological challenge: impact of communist thought
Changing human attitudes: art and literature in the contemporary world
Source: Introduction to Contemporary History (C.A. Watts, 1964).

Humanities Curriculum Project

War and society
Education
The family
Relations between the sexes
Poverty
People and work
Living in cities
Law and order
(Race relations)
Source: Introduction to Humanities Curriculum Project (Heinemann, 1970).

One World Trust

World food and population
Colonialism
Race relations
Conflict and its resolution
Organs of world co-operation
Source: World Questions: A Study Guide (ed. Henderson) (Methuen, 1963).

transferable. These are the arguments put forward, for example, by
Holloway (in Burston and Thompson 1967), but immediately attacked
by historians, such as Burston, on the grounds that such an approach is
too concerned with the present and with erecting a model — at the
expense of the study of the past, the particular, and especially the
human particular. More recent essays, however, have begun to argue the
case for complementarity rather than exclusiveness. This has been
perhaps most clearly put by an historian, Derek Heater. He sees
social science concepts as 'providing ways of articulating the historical
modes of thought' in their ability to provide a frame for comparative
analysis.[8] So, he goes on: 'fusing the two groups of subjects . . . history

provides the variety and colour of its narrative and biographical matter while the social sciences provide a coherent learning structure' (1970: 141) (see Chart 5).

The fact that such frameworks are more naturally 'integrative' than the thematic has meant that such approaches have proved popular, not only for teaching twentieth-century history,[9] but for framing a whole curriculum in the humanities. Teachers interested in such approaches will find two recently published handbooks by Lawton and Dufour (1973) and Mathias (1973) very helpful not only for practical reference and syllabus design, but also for their broader theoretical rationales.[10]

For history teaching proper, however, the advantages and drawbacks of the approach are substantially the same as for the thematic approach – those of 'present-mindedness' and 'model-building'. Practice has shown the latter to be the more significant perhaps because of the emphasis upon concepts rather than case studies. Certainly too great an emphasis in this direction can again devalue the human context – which is the history teacher's central concern. Once again it is the 'value of the subject' which is in question.[11]

OTHER NEW APPROACHES

(1) *Towards world history*

The last two illustrations have tried to show the way in which the nature of twentieth-century history has led teachers to alter their approach to syllabus making. If the fastest growing field in history teaching in the last decade has been that of the twentieth century, it is also inspiring more teachers to think in terms of a complete world history syllabus – to reinterpret 'heritage' in a holistic sense. Within two years of publishing *Towards World History* in 1967, the DES thought it necessary to attempt a complete revision and updating.[12] If the immediate motivation derives from the desire to explain the present, it goes further. The 'shaping forces of our time', the expanding mushroom of contemporary world history, need to be supported on something rather more substantial than the slender stalk of the 'island' story – particularly if the demand for social education is given any weight. James Henderson has been the most eloquent advocate of the theme that the age of one world must give some introduction to awareness of the 'timeless cultural deposits of other civilisations'. His point is reinforced by Grousset who shows how comparative a late comer is Western Europe in his *Sum of History*.[13] In other words the island story is simply too narrow a view of heritage.

The fundamental point is that unlike any of the other approaches discussed above the teacher has to be the pioneer. As the last chapter

Chart 5   A SOCIAL SCIENCE FRAMEWORK FOR TWENTIETH CENTURY HISTORY (Using concepts in political science)

	Russian Revolution	Versailles Settlement	Nazism	Second World War	Cold War	USA since 1945	India	Africa	UNO	Modern Britain
Leadership	Lenin		Hitler	Churchill		Kennedy	Gandhi	Nkrumah	Hammarskjold	
Decision-making	Seizure of power			War cabinet		Cuban missile crisis			Security council and the veto	Comprehensive schools
Role of the individual					CND	Civil Rights movement				General election
Ideology	Communism	National self-determination	Nazism				Hinduism v. Islam	Apartheid		
International conflict				German and Japanese wars	Cuban missile crisis	Vietnamese war				Suez crisis
Resolution of international conflict		Peace settlement			Test-ban agreement			Decolonisation	Congo	

Source: D. Heater (1970) 'History and the Social Sciences', in M. Ballard (ed.), *New Movements in the Study and Teaching of History* (London, Temple Smith), p. 144.

illustrated, any attempt to write a world history by professional historians has always aroused a bitter controversy. Not only is the teacher alone but the other aims relating to this approach are at their vaguest — how does one make precise a meaning for 'improving international understanding'? At the same time world history is obviously the extreme case in syllabus-making, where interpretations of the criteria of importance in selection and suitability for teaching are being stretched to their limits.

In this position no single approach can hope to answer every individual view or need. Two problems are perhaps worth illustrating in detail. The first is the need to provide a clear frame of interpretation, when faced with the breadth and time scale of selection involved. Here a series of ILEA teacher conferences (1969, 1970) have offered very helpful insights. Their task was to compare the values of chronological, thematic and area treatments against the particular problems of chronology and breadth. The important and unanimous conclusion was that, whichever approach was adopted, the clearest teaching framework was provided by a perspective based on the idea of development. This was seen as consisting of three stages: 'Man learns to live in Society', 'Pre-Industrial Society' and 'Industrial Society'. The teachers saw this perspective as being able to illustrate the historian's concern with change and continuity but, since all these types of society also existed in the contemporary world, it would be possible to move comparatively backwards and forwards in time and so avoid an evolutionary attitude towards 'progress' in development. It was argued that this approach could be used even in a 'chronological' syllabus, though the other treatments developed it more clearly in showing that understanding of the range of man's experience (areas) or the growing variety of his needs (themes) can be as important towards understanding historical experience as grasping evolution across time.[14]

The second point highlighted by these syllabuses is the way selection embodied the inquiry approach. This was again based on case studies, and made much use of the social science disciplines. The essential difference to the earlier social science example, however, lay in the insistence that the concepts be subordinated to an overall perspective of change, a difference which it was hoped would allow for a greater development of the narrative element so important to history.

The other consideration in any world history interpretation is the place of national history. This is where the work of a second group, teacher-fellows of the School of Oriental and African Studies, is complementary to that of the ILEA. If this group's approach appears less adventurous, it is nevertheless interesting for the way in which a developing perspective of national history is related to wider concerns (SOAS 1973).

(2) *The evidential approach and the discontinuous syllabus*

The final suggestion for a recasting of the conventional approach to syllabus design is to be found in the writing of D.G. Watts (1972) and in the experimental syllabus at present being developed by the Schools Council History 13-16 Project Team, led by David Sylvester. It is termed the discontinuous syllabus. Both Watts and Sylvester emphasise that encouraging the involvement and interest of both pupil and teacher is their main concern. This advocacy of suitability is related to the notion of importance when they argue that syllabus design should be based on sampling the various activities and areas within the subject, as opposed to absorbing any single or continuous perspective. (Indeed the Schools Council project also states as an explicit aim that, for those teachers who see chronology as a basic constraint, such a syllabus would enable them to achieve their freedom!)

The difference between the two suggestions is between theory and practice and age range. Watts' writing antedates the Schools Council Project and covers the whole curriculum. He argues that history teaching should adopt a three-stage approach. That for the lower junior age range will be based on 'familiar stories which introduce opportunities to identify with people in the past'. The next stage takes a 'socialising viewpoint'; while its main emphasis is on British history it is also intended to introduce units on Europe and the wider world. Within this there are two linking ideas. First, to develop a sense of time. Here Watts suggests that particular societies should continually reappear in order to make clear to the pupils how they develop and to encourage a relative understanding of chronology. The second theme is the emphasis on causation. Watts feels that, if the illustrations are chosen to move both forwards and then backwards in time, the pupils should be able to develop some feeling for, and appreciation of, cause and effect.

Watts' suggestions have yet to be translated into practice. By contrast the Schools Council Project syllabus is already undergoing trials and, as was said earlier, is geared to terminal examinations at CSE and 'O' level. The syllabus (see Chart 6) contrasts a local study with a developmental topic — medicine, while the patch studies embrace both such well-worked topics as the American West and challenging issues in contemporary history, such as the Arab-Israeli conflict. As the Project's work is still incomplete it is impossible to speculate upon its effects upon either pupil-interest or teacher-thinking. However, it is worth emphasising that the move away from conventional patterns is being pressed by the first national history project. The general point from both these illustrations is the encouragement they offer the teacher to explore and develop his own interpretation of history, creating his own synthesis of the variety of purposes and different types of explanation embraced by the subject.

Chart 6   A DISCONTINUOUS SYLLABUS (for a two-year course and examination in history at GCE/CSE level)

FRAMEWORK OF SYLLABUS	CONTENT	SUGGESTED TEACHING TIME 3 HOURS A WEEK (4-5 PERIODS)
STUDY IN DEVELOPMENT (A study of the factors affecting the development of a topic through time.)	Medicine	1 Term
INQUIRY IN DEPTH (Study of aspects of a period of the past involving imaginative reconstruction and contrast with the present and also a biographical study showing the interrelation of a person to his times.)	One of the following: Renaissance Italy 1450-1500 (Leonardo da Vinci) Elizabethan England 1558-1603 (Mary Queen of Scots) Britain 1815-1851 (Shaftesbury) The American West 1846-1890 (Theodore Roosevelt)	1½ Terms
STUDIES IN MODERN WORLD HISTORY (Three studies on modern issues viewed historically.)	The Rise of Communist China The Move to European Unity Arab-Israeli Conflict	1½ Terms
HISTORY AROUND US (A study of the history around us, using the visible evidence as the starting point. This will involve visits to sites.)	One of the following: Prehistoric Britain Roman Britain Castles & Fortified Houses 1066-1550 Country Houses 1550-1800 Church Buildings and Furnishings 1066-1900 The Making of the Landscape Town Development and Domestic Architecture 1700 to the Present Aspects of the History of the Locality	1 Term

Reproduced by permission of the Schools Council from Schools Council project *History 13-16*, Newsletter 1, April 1973.

CONCLUSION: THE DISCONTINUOUS SYLLABUS AS THE TREND
FOR THE FUTURE

This style of syllabus making offers an appropriate note upon which to
end a chapter which has attempted to survey the main approaches to
selection. It is important to reiterate that no one approach is argued as
being better than the next. What is being stressed are the different
priorities that the approaches place upon aims. The other conclusion is
that a common feature across all the approaches is the attempt to gain
greater interest and involvement from the pupils through introducing
them to more 'realistic' historical experiences. The need is to temper
the claims of importance with those of suitability — the subject of the
next chapter.

NOTES

1. See E.H. Dance (1970) *The Place of History in Secondary
   Teaching: A Comparative Study* (London, Harrap).
2. Cambridge History Teaching Today Group (Cambridge Institute
   of Education, 1970), pp. 7-12.
3. See Giles (1973).
4. In Burston (1971) *Principles of History Teaching* (London,
   Methuen), chapters 6 and 7, and Burston and Green (eds.) (1972)
   Handbook for History Teachers (London, Methuen), chapter 5.
5. See chapter 3.
6. The book in question is E.P. Thompson's (1963) *The Making of
   the English Working Class* (London, Gollancz).
7. See Holley (1974).
8. Heater has extended this analysis more generally in his later
   article 'The Social Sciences and History: A Model for Integration',
   in *General Education* (1972), no. 18, pp. 25-8.
9. An even more recent example of this trend is to be found in the
   Open University third level course, *Historical Data and the Social
   Sciences*, D301, Units 1-4, *The Quantitative Analysis of Historical
   Data* (Open University, 1974).
10. See Chapter 6.
11. There has been considerable debate on this in the development of
    the Oxford 'O' level sociology examination, where the examiners'
    concern for knowledge of the 'language' of the discipline has
    contrasted with the teachers' aim to motivate their pupils'
    interest in the subject.
12. Still to be published!
13. R. Grousset, *Sum of History* (1951) (Trans. A. and H. Temple
    Patterson, Tower Bridge Publications).
14. See ILEA Conference Reports and Appendix of syllabus frame-
    works developed by Islay Doncaster.

BIBLIOGRAPHY

BALLARD, M. (ed.) (1970) *New Movements in the Study and Teaching of History* (London, Temple Smith).

BARRACLOUGH, G. (1967) *History and the Common Man* (London, Historical Association).

BRYANT, Margaret E. (1967) 'The History Syllabus Reconsidered', in *History in the Secondary School* (London, Historical Association).

____(1970) 'Documentary and Study Materials for Teachers and Pupils', in *Teaching History,* vol. 1, no. 3, pp. 194-202; vol. 2, no. 4, pp. 272-8.

____(1971) 'Documentary and Study Materials for Teachers and Pupils', in *Teaching History,* vol. 2, no. 5, pp. 35-47.

____(1972) 'General and Aspect History', in Burston and Green (1972).

BRYANT, Margaret E. and ECCLESTONE, G. (1968) *World Outlook 1900-1965: Class Workbook* (London, Faber).

BURSTON, W.H. and GREEN, C.W. (eds.) (1972) *Handbook for History Teachers* (London, Methuen, rev. edn).

CARPENTER, P. (1964) *The Era Approach* Cambridge, CUP).

CHAFFER, J.M. (1973) 'What History Should We Teach?' in Jones, R.B. (1973), pp. 47-83.

CHINNERY, G.A. (1970) *Studying Urban History in Schools* (London, Historical Association).

DES (1967) *Towards World History* (London, HMSO).

DOUCH, R. (1967) *Local History and the Teacher* (London, Routledge). See also 'Local History' in Burston and Green (1972) and Ballard (1970).

FAIRLEY, J.S. (1970) *Patch History and Creativity* (Harlow, Longmans).

FINES, J. (1970) *The History Teacher and Other Disciplines* (London, Historical Association).

GILES, Phyllis (1973) 'History in the Secondary School: A Survey', in *Journal of Curriculum Studies,* vol. 5, pp. 133-44.

GILES, Phyllis and NEAL, G. (1973) 'History Teaching Analysed', in *Trends in Education,* no. 32, pp. 16-25.

HEATER, D. (1970) 'History and the Social Sciences', in Ballard (1970), pp. 134-45.

HENDERSON, J.L. (1966) *World Questions: A Study Guide* (London, Methuen).

____(1972) 'World History', in Burston and Green (1972), pp. 90-9.

____ *Teaching History,* see also vol. 1, no. 1 (1969) pp. 8-11 and no. 2 (1969), pp. 103-8 for annotated bibliographies on twentieth century world history.

HILL, C.P. (1953) *Towards World Understanding, No. IX, Suggestions on the Teaching of History* (London, UNESCO).

HOLLEY, B.J. (1974) *A-Level Syllabus Studies: History and Physics* (London, Macmillan, Schools Council Research Studies).

INNER LONDON EDUCATION AUTHORITY (1969) 'Towards A World History Syllabus for the First Three Years of Secondary School' (internally distributed).

___(1970) 'Towards a World History Syllabus for the 4th, 5th and 6th Years of Secondary School' (internally distributed).

JEFFREYS, M.V.C. (1939) *History in Schools: the Study of Development* (London, Pitman).

JONES, R.B. (1973) *Practical Approaches to the New History* (London, Hutchinson).

LAMONT, W. (ed.) (1972) *The Realities of Teaching History: Beginnings* (London, Chatto & Windus).

LYALL, Anthea (1967) *History Syllabuses in a World Perspective* (Harlow, Longmans).

SCHOOLS COUNCIL (April 1973). *History 13-16, Newsletter.*

SCHOOL OF ORIENTAL AND AFRICAN STUDIES (1973) *World History Secondary School Syllabuses.* This also contains a useful annotated bibliography.

STEEL, D.J. and TAYLOR, L. (1973) *Family History in Schools* (Chichester, Phillimore).

THOMSON, D. (1969) *The Aims of History* (London, Thames & Hudson).

TURNER, D. (1971) *Historical Demography in Schools* (London, Historical Association).

WATTS, D.G. (1972) *Learning of History* (London, Routledge).

Chapter 3

How Should We Teach History?

New methods and better understanding?

> We kill by conscientiousness. We feel an obligation to impart informa-
> tion from the highest of motives: we feel that we have failed our
> children somehow if they have not heard of 'Old Luther and that
> sort of thing'. We feel that we can reconcile this aim with our other
> aims – involving our children with figures from the past and
> instilling in them a sense of curiosity and romance – and we are not
> sufficiently honest in acknowledging to ourselves how often, in
> pursuing one goal, we subvert the other.

> W. Lamont (ed.) (1972) *The Realities of History Teaching*
> (London, Chatto & Windus), p. 160.

The teacher who set out six principles which would underlie the new
syllabus he wished to draw up would command much support.
1. It must be child-centred as opposed to the traditional method of
   a body of knowledge that must be learned.
2. It must be relevant to the children and their situation in this day
   and age.
3. Fewer topics must be studied in greater depth.
4. The child must become involved – perhaps the most important
   point.
5. Historical method, thinking and attitudes will be more important
   than facts.
6. It must come up to the present by the end of the third year.

> Cambridge History Teaching Today Group (1970) *The
> Teaching of History to the 11-14 Age Group* (Cambridge
> Institute of Education), p.17.

Teachers tend to begin by considering what content they want to teach
but, for the pupil, is not *how* they teach it more important? This is to
highlight 'suitability' or to put the pupil before the subject – perhaps
the first priority. The previous chapter outlined the variety in current
approaches and stressed the urgent need for agreement on criteria for
selection. This one sets the growing concern for effective teaching
techniques in the context of the developing knowledge of the pupil's
capabilities and limitations in learning. Have not teachers always been
perplexed by their pupils' confused sense of time, by their muddled
explanations and the difficulties they find in organising arguments?

Teachers have tended to be sceptical of the classroom application of educational research, yet all these problems can now be analysed much more clearly as a result. This point is reinforced by the conclusion of the Cambridgeshire report that 'history is not keeping pace with the new methods now being adopted in other subjects'. Briefly, history teachers are now faced by the practical need to develop more flexible learning strategies because curriculum reform has secured a general acceptance for the enquiry-approach and because mixed ability grouping has become widespread as a result of comprehensive reorganisation. Both of these also point to the further need to take account of group interaction in learning. So the first part of this chapter examines three questions:

What major problems arise for the history teacher in trying to *interpret* and *communicate* his subject?
How far should the *psychological readiness* of the pupil influence this process?
How far can *grouping techniques* help the learning process?

Of course, history teachers have not ignored such developments, as a comparison of the general article on psychology in the 1962 *Handbook for History Teachers* with the much more specific discussion of 'some psychological aspects' in the 1972 revision shows. The second section of the chapter therefore discusses how writers and present approaches have been influenced by these developments.

PSYCHOLOGICAL PROBLEMS OF LEARNING HISTORY

(1) *Time concepts*
As the last chapter brought out, chronology is usually the first problem to be faced in syllabus making. The trend has been to reject a rigid framework yet the relative value of some time sense cannot be disputed. Would not history without time be like the emperor without his clothes? Perhaps few teachers today realise just how far back the debate can be traced? It can be found in Barnes (1904) and was publicised by Oakden and Sturt's research in the twenties.[1] The starting point for contemporary discussion however can be dated from Jahoda's essay (1963) which summarised all previous findings. This emphasised that most adolescent pupils could not grasp the useful meaning behind a date — for them history was 'one damn thing after another'. The subsequent studies this inspired have all reinforced this general conclusion though from a variety of viewpoints; it is now agreed that the pupil's grasp of the time scale reflected in words like 'century' or by comparing dates is not reached until about sixteen.

There has been a good deal of other research on questions of chronology but this does not seem particularly helpful here. (For example, the controversy over 'earlier means easier' shows itself more to be a problem of communication; the teacher's wish to transmit ideas and feelings about the past to pupils' limitations in being able to grasp them. The real need is for tangible evidence or the ability to create imaginative involvement — a past with which the pupils can identify, as in John Fines' use of drama.[2]) Whether or not teachers have been directly influenced by this research there is surely a noticeable trend in current syllabuses towards a more relative chronology — to be able to order and re-order dates, rather than to simply recall them. (Vikainen's research[3] suggests that the development of this time sense can be accelerated, but other writers argue that this will be achieved only at the expense of other ends. The question is one of balance. How absolute is the importance of developing a time sense in history teaching?)

(2) *Conceptual developments*
Perhaps a more important effect of the research into chronology has been to catalyse interest in parallel problems — such as the limited or confused nature of most pupils' attempts at 'explanation'. This is a question of conceptual capability which depends on two other factors: the pupil's capacity to think logically and his ability to understand and use language — particularly the specialised vocabulary so often employed by the teacher and the textbook.

(3) *Logical thinking*
The importance of Piaget's work on the development of logical think-ing in the 1920s is that it was popularised in the 1950s and has since provided the model to be applied to the problems of teaching and learning in other disciplines. The novel thesis he advanced was that development occurred in three main stages: pre-operational, concrete and formal. The first is the stage at which the child relies upon his own intuitive reasoning; the second is where his understanding is developing to the point where he can master those ideas or problems which he can represent physically; the final stage is the ability to handle ideas in the abstract and, in Piaget's view, is generally achieved by the age of fourteen.

In history teaching the best known research has been that by Peel (1960), Coltham (1960), Hallam (1967) and Stones (1967). The significance of their various studies is that they extend the earlier research on time by suggesting that in history the formal stage is generally only achieved by sixteen. An illustration of this is found in Peel's experiments where he asked a group of pupils aged seven to sixteen to 'interpret' an aerial photograph of Stonehenge. To the questions:

'Do you think Stonehenge might have been a fort and not a temple?'
and 'Why do you think that?'
A seven-year old answered:
'*A temple.*' 'Why?' '*Because people live in it.*'
At nine the answer becomes more elaborate:
'*I think it might have been to stop the enemy charging through.*'
'Why do you think so?' '*It looks like it. The bricks would stand up.
The enemy could not force through quick enough and they'd be
killed.*'
At fourteen the answer shows a much greater sense of logic:
'*I think it would be a temple because it has a round formation with
an altar at the top end, and at a certain time of the year the sun
shines straight up a path towards the altar, and I think that it was
used for the worship of the sun god. There was no roof on it so
that the sun shines right into the temple. There is a lot of hard work
and labour in it for a god and the fact that they brought the blue
stone from Wales.*'
(1960, 118-19.)

(4) *Language*

Does not this example also highlight, almost as a parallel problem, the
use and understanding of language? Research into both teachers' use
and pupils' grasp of language has been more recent but has shown how
important this is in helping to clarify understanding of learning. There
are two strands here: first, awareness of the general problems of the
restricted and elaborated codes raised by Bernstein (1965) and secondly,
increasing awareness of children's difficulty in understanding the
context of words, particularly the specialised vocabulary used by the
history teacher. Barnes' *Language, the Learner and the School* is the
best known example, but a good illustration is afforded by Jeanette
Coltham's (1960) research into younger pupils' connotations of
commonly used words in history teaching: the word 'law', for example,
is equated by most eleven-year-old pupils with the term 'rule', as the
only experience available to them. The wider historical meaning of
statute law is only realised very slowly.

(5) *The nature of concepts*

From his illustration Peel draws the distinction between a 'descriptive'
and an 'explanatory' response. It is an argument which highlights the
way in which knowledge of conceptual development is the link
between understanding the pupil and selecting content in syllabus
design; the history teacher has to consider not only the 'suitability'
of the concepts he has to teach but also their 'importance'. For
example, how important is it to know about Stonehenge or Luther?

The choice of these surely depends on their association with periods or eras – how far is the 'New Stone Age' or the 'Reformation' the essential idea to be grasped? Yet to fully understand either surely involves a grasp of more general concepts; for example, of notions of Church and State. To what extent are these the essential ideas to be communicated because, though particular to the specific cases, they are important to developing general historical understanding? Lastly, teachers' aims also reflect deep concern to communicate some interpretative framework based on perceptions of change and continuity, cause and effect. What relationship do such abstract 'organising' ideas have in this scale of 'importance'?

It is such questions which relate research to practice. They are posed as questions because there is as yet little research to guide conclusions. The London Institute has made some tentative studies of the first, while the Schools Council History, Geography and Social Science Project 8-13 has suggested the possibility of a syllabus founded on 'key concepts' at the fourth level. The only pertinent models have been American, those by Taba and Bruner. Though aimed at clarifying approaches in social studies rather than history alone, the propositions of these two psychologists are of great value because their conclusions are testable in the two curricula which they have inspired.[4] The main concern for both is to mediate the aims of a knowledge-based curriculum to basic considerations of child development.

As Taba explains in the introduction to her curriculum handbooks:

> *Originally, those involved in developing this curriculum design struggled with the conflict between the coverage, or the broadening scope, in the social studies curriculum and the demands for greater depth. From this struggle came the theoretical foundation for the new approach to curriculum development. First, it becomes clear that the subject matter had to be seen as consisting of three levels of knowledge, each of which served a special function in curriculum organisation and learning: (1) the key concepts that serve as threads weaving through many grade levels; (2) the significant ideas that serve as focal points for the selection and organisation of the content and represent the fundamental learnings; and (3) the specific facts and cases that serve as samples through the analysis of which students could arrive at the important ideas. (1971: iii-iv.)*

These levels were related through the notion of 'key concepts'. The importance of these concepts is that they are 'highly abstract generalisations selected from the social sciences for their power to organise and synthesise large numbers of relationships, specific facts and ideas' (1971). Such difficult ideas were to be mediated through introducing them in simple, concrete and familiar contexts 'spiralling' outwards to a wider framework (see Chart 7).

Chart 7 THE SPIRAL DEVELOPMENT OF THREE KEY CONCEPTS

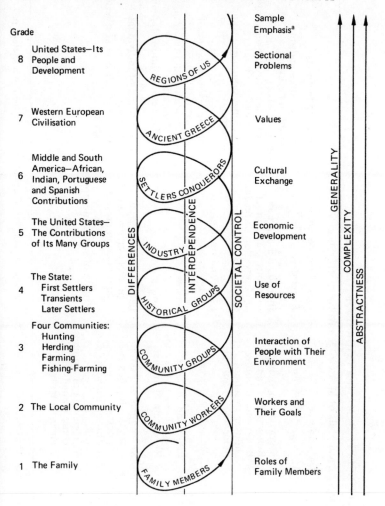

Source: Hilda Taba *et al.* (1971) *A Teacher's Handbook to Elementary Social Studies* (California, Addison Wesley), p. 21.

Bruner has embodied Taba's approach in a general statement. He argues that any theory of instruction should have two hall-marks: a coherent theory of learning linked to a progressive structure. The prime merit of a structure is that it should be capable of 'simplifying information for generating new propositions and for

Chart 8 TEACHING CONCEPTS IN MAN: A COURSE OF STUDY

The conceptual and pedagogical goals of M.A.C.O.S. involve specifically:

Conceptual Themes	Data Sources	Classroom Techniques	Learning Methods
Life cycle (including reproduction)	1. *Primary Sources*	*Examples*	Enquiry, investigation (problem-defining, hypothesising, experimentation, observation, interviewing, literature searching, summarising and reporting)
Adaptation	Student experiences Behaviour of family Behaviour of young children in school Behaviour of animals	Individual and group research, e.g. direct observation or reading of texts	
Learning			
Aggression		Large and small group discussion	Sharing and evaluating of interpretation
Organisation of groups (including group relationships, the family and community, division of labour)	2. *Secondary Sources* Films and slides of animals and Eskimos Recording of animal sounds	Games	Accumulating and retaining information
		Role play	Exchange of opinion, defence of opinion
Technology	Recordings of Eskimo myths, legends and poetry Anthropological field notes	Large and small group projects such as art and construction projects	Exploration of individual feelings
Communication and language	Written data on humans, other animals and environments	Writing of songs and poems	Exposure to diverse aesthetic styles
World view			
Values			

Source: Educational Development Centre (1970) *Man: A Course of Study* (Washington, Curriculum Development Associates), p. 7.

increasing the manipulability of a body of knowledge' (1966:41).
Through such a 'courteous translation' Bruner argues that 'any subject
can be taught in some intellectually honest form to any child at any
stage of development' (1963: 33). It is these assertions and their
translation into a curriculum – *Man: A Course of Study* (1970) –
which have so interested writers on both psychology and the curriculum
ever since (see Chart 8).

SOCIAL INTERACTION: LEARNING AND TEACHING METHODS

This research has also generated interest in new teaching and learning
strategies. Piaget, Taba and Bruner have all emphasised the value of
co-operation in learning, a point which the classroom implications of
primary and comprehensive organisation now underline. So much
greater value is now being placed on discussion and question posing.
The aim is to encourage motivation through pupil participation in
articulating both his findings and his own feelings. More important, it
is felt that discussion helps him to realise the value of his contributions
by relating and comparing them to those of his peers.[5] The other result
is that teachers are beginning to appreciate the value of research into
the social psychology of teaching, particularly questions of pupil-
pupil and teacher-pupil interaction in the classroom.[6] These highlight
the need for teachers to understand more fully the dynamics of the
classroom, of working both with groups of pupils and also collabora-
tively with their colleagues.

On the first of these, Fairley (1967: 79-84) is the only author who
has raised the issue specifically for history teaching. His arguments,
however, are very generalised and derivative from the work of Moreno.[7]
Kaye and Rogers' (1968) approach is perhaps more useful in that they
offer a more detailed analysis of the general problem of group learning.
Their conclusion is that the formation of groups should depend on the
interest shared in a particular project rather than reasons of social
compatibility. This appears a more flexible approach because it allows
grouping to follow the interests of the class and so is more likely to
maintain motivation.

The parallel development that needs to be mentioned here has been
that of team teaching. Its usual aim has been to make optimum use of
the range of interests and specialist skills amongst any group of teachers.
The immediate problem highlighted by writers such as Freeman (1969)
and Warwick (1971) has been one of definition. Although little writing
is specific to history teaching, most of the approaches described relate
to the humanities. Warwick's analysis (1971 : Chapter 10) offers perhaps
the most practical introduction to the range of considerations to be
faced in developing such a team situation (see Chart 9). However
one possible danger in his analysis is its optimism, because experience

Chart 9 DEVELOPING TEAM TEACHING

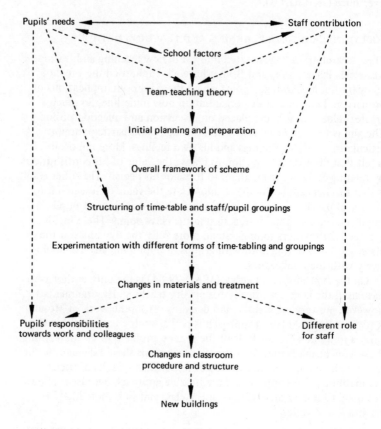

Source: D. Warwick (1971), *Team Teaching* (London ULP), p. 115

has shown that the most successful team work has usually only developed where there has been a stable core of teachers supported by a reasonable level of resources.[8]

THEORY INTO PRACTICE

Hallam (1970) has drawn attention to the need for a rational balance. If the presentation of the traditional approach was obviously at fault, the contemporary emphasis on enquiry has equally often been very loosely interpreted; the 'match' has to be very carefully worked out. So this section considers three further questions:

How widely have such research findings been communicated?
How do they inform new approaches?
What implications, if any, are there for the future?

Two trends are discernible: motivation through enquiry — 'learning by doing', and, secondly, introducing the pupil to the discipline of history — an approach which hinges on interpreting evidence.

(1) *Motivation through enquiry*

'The curriculum is to be thought of in terms of activity and experience rather than of knowledge to be acquired and facts to be stored.' This is the shibboleth of the enquiry approach which echoes back from Plowden in 1967 to Hadow in 1931 and Dewey's advocacy of the heuristic. The approach has most successfully rooted in the primary school and there are obvious practical reasons for this. First, the removal of the eleven-plus has allowed primary schools real freedom to determine their curriculum — in sharp contrast to the secondary sector. As a result teachers have been able to explore pupils' interests and needs much more individually, both because of the strong class-teacher tradition and because there is no need to constrain enquiry to narrow subject boundaries. Given this encouragement teachers have shown great sensitivity in their understanding of the ways in which pupils' potential can be encouraged.[9] However, though this approach chimes well with psychological advocacy, its supporters have often been naive in their optimism for 'openness'. This is shown by the present trend towards achieving a balance between 'interests' and 'needs' and the attempt to define the essential skills and concepts which ought to be realised at this level.

The pragmatic emphasis is well demonstrated by Rance (1968). His summary of the advantages of the enquiry approach is generalised: 'as placing the main emphasis upon the child rather than on the subject'; encouraging him 'to construct his own method of approach to knowledge'; the provision of opportunities 'to learn how to learn'; the 'breaking down of subject barriers, even though the starting point for the main theme may be provided by an academic subject'; the necessity of allowing a child to acquire knowledge through natural curiosity about his environment. The main values of his book lie in its distinctions between the different kinds of study — project, centre of interest, environmental or topic — and the detailed, practical analysis of organisational needs.

The middle years have to reflect the transition from such an 'open' curriculum towards one which is 'subject centred'.[10] Here Fairley's *Patch History and Creativity* is an interesting example of such a bridge. While following the idea of a historical patch, he shows how its boundaries can be extended to show creative and imaginative dimensions.

At the secondary level Sheila Ferguson's (1968) suggestions for encouraging motivation and interest through teaching with projects are now familiar and have been restated in her article in Ballard (1970). However, in the light of developments since then, her arguments may strike many teachers as being too generalised. She does not go as far as Peter Carpenter in discussion of group work, nor as far as Margaret Bryant in discussing the possible range of original and source materials.[11] Again her view that the project should be only subordinate and supplementary: 'to avoid superficiality, lack of system and of intellectual discipline', may not be acceptable.

In fact Milne (1973: 133) has provided a much wider rationale for the project method. For him the key criterion is the concept of historical 'validity'. To illustrate this he cites an extreme case, a project which focuses on the music of Chopin. If Chopin's work is used 'to support a broader theme or if the music is explained by reference to the composer's historical environment' it is valid; if it is 'immersed in the music to the exclusion of all else' it is not. Other aims cited as desirable and analysed in the essay are those of insight, evaluation, analysis and creativity. This emphasis on the need to define aims is also made in the Southern Regional Examination Board's pamphlet on projects: 'unless there is a clear path from the aims of project work through to its assessment there will inevitably be an educational mis-match and the value of work will be much reduced' (p. 9). To avoid losing sight of aims and to monitor progress systematically the Board suggests the use of project control charts.

At the sixth form level an interesting approach to evidential methods has been developed by the General Studies Project in GILTS (Guided Individual Learning in Tutorials and Seminars). The Project's materials are produced as units designed 'as an hour's work for an average sixth former'. Each contains a guide to the selected topic, together with a collection of evidence articulating contrasting opinions or interpretations. These are supported by further book references and a teacher's note. In this way the project is stimulating the development of an evidential approach and one which also puts a new emphasis on learning and discussion at the pupil's own level. (The project also makes the point that such units can be used in subject teaching just as easily as for general studies.)

(2) *Motivation through evidence*

John Fines' advocacy of the potential use of archive and documentary evidence even for the junior school is now well known. However, a more specific analysis of the objectives to be met in such work is to be found in Margaret Bryant's surveys in *Teaching History* (1970). She distinguishes three purposes for which an historian may use such evidence:

> That of illuminating or presenting an established narrative or exposition;
> Of supporting, justifying, modifying or criticising it;
> Or of constructing a new narrative, analysis, synthesis.

She concedes that 'teachers may justifiably pursue all three' but that to translate them into educational objectives needs 'caution and humility'. Her conclusions follow those already argued in the previous section and show the way in which educational research can positively help a teacher towards achievement. The other way in which evidence is increasingly being used is through the development of explanations using 'aspect' history, as described in the previous chapter.

(3) *Concepts and understanding*

The problem of defining the types of concepts that history teachers should seek to develop has already been discussed. This section is concerned with how these might be approached in practice. Here Pollard's (1973) account of a local study in Swindon shows a good general awareness of the range of understandings; the strands of chronology, community and evidence. Steel and Taylor's *Family History in Schools* has gone further. Two chapters are devoted to refining the implications in developing such understanding (and in their forthcoming 'main-line programme' these are expanded to form a basis for the whole, (see Chart 10). However, all these are limited approaches, segmental in their application. Watts' book (1972) offers a well argued rationale in similar terms for the whole curriculum — this, however, is still theory. The only working examples are the Bruner and Taba curricula described above and in Chapter 6.

CONCLUSION

'The antithesis of content and methods of enquiry is, up to a point, a false one. No teaching of content in the past has ever excluded the possibility of the pupil's developing historical skills; no teaching of a mode of enquiry can exist in a vacuum, and the skills will have to be exercised on an area of content' (Lamont, 1970: 167).

History, psychology and sociology are 'segments'. The need is to link them and to fit them into a whole — to achieve a synthesis which is sensitive and flexible enough to respond quickly to every advance in

Chart 10 FAMILY HISTORY PROJECT

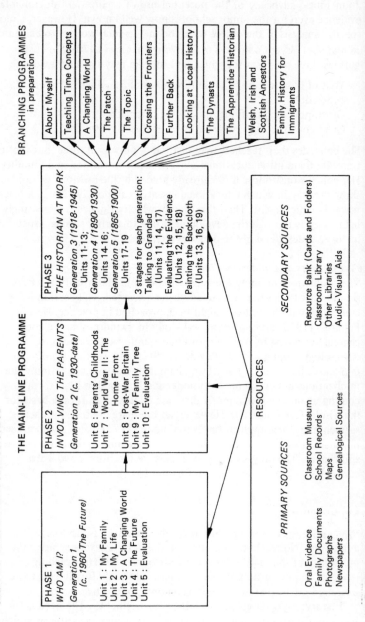

THE MAIN-LINE PROGRAMME

BRANCHING PROGRAMMES
in preparation

- About Myself
- Teaching Time Concepts
- A Changing World
- The Patch
- The Topic
- Crossing the Frontiers
- Further Back
- Looking at Local History
- The Dynasts
- The Apprentice Historian
- Welsh, Irish and Scottish Ancestors
- Family History for Immigrants

PHASE 1
WHO AM I?
Generation 1
(c. 1960–The Future)

Unit 1 : My Family
Unit 2 : My Life
Unit 3 : A Changing World
Unit 4 : The Future
Unit 5 : Evaluation

PHASE 2
INVOLVING THE PARENTS
Generation 2 (c. 1930–date)

Unit 6 : Parents' Childhoods
Unit 7 : World War II: The Home Front
Unit 8 : Post-War Britain
Unit 9 : My Family Tree
Unit 10 : Evaluation

PHASE 3
THE HISTORIAN AT WORK
Generation 3 (1918–1945)
Units 11-13:
Generation 4 (1890-1930)
Units 14-16:
Generation 5 (1865-1900)
Units 17-19

3 stages for each generation:
Talking to Grandad
(Units 11, 14, 17)
Evaluating the Evidence
(Units 12, 15, 18)
Painting the Backcloth
(Units 13, 16, 19)

RESOURCES

PRIMARY SOURCES

Oral Evidence
Family Documents
Photographs
Newspapers
Classroom Museum
School Records
Maps
Genealogical Sources

SECONDARY SOURCES

Resource Bank (Cards and Folders)
Classroom Library
Other Libraries
Audio-Visual Aids

teaching and learning. Is not the teacher the person who is most directly involved in all three? Might he not be the best qualified to develop such a synthesis — to define what is possible in terms of what is desirable?

NOTES

1. See M.S. Barnes (1904) *Studies in Historical Method* (Boston) and E.C. Oakden and M. Sturt, 'The Development of the Knowledge of Time in Children', in *British Journal of Psychology*, vol.12, part 4 (1922), pp. 309-36.

2. See J. Fines and R. Verrier, (1974) *The Drama of History* (Bingley).

3. See 'The Development of Time Concepts and Time Schemes' (Turku Institute of Education, Finland, 1961).

4. See *Taba Social Studies Curriculum* (1971) and *Man: A Course of Study* (1970).

5. See discussion of Humanities Curriculum Project, Chapter 6, pp. 102-3.

6. The way in which such concern is also beginning to affect tertiary education is illustrated by the Small Group Discussion project led by Jean Rudduck, Centre for Applied Research into Education, University of East Anglia and financed by the University Grants Committee.

7. A brief critique of sociometric techniques as applied to the classroom can be found in Richardson (1973: 50-1).

8. E. Richardson (1973), *The Teacher, the School and the Task of Management*, provides a comprehensive discussion of many of the problems involved.

9. 'Children are full of physical energy and love to be active. They are immensely curious about their surroundings. They like being together and they like talking. They are interested in people and what people have to do, in things and how things work. They have considerable powers of imagination in relation to people and events. They are not self-conscious and have a quick gift for play acting.' (Edinburgh, Moray House: 1965, 2)

10. See Schools Council, (1969) *The Middle Years of Schooling 8-13; Working Paper 22* (HMSO) and A.M. Ross *et al.* (1972) *Education in the Middle Years: Working Paper 42* (London, Evans).

11. See bibliography.

BIBLIOGRAPHY

Research

BALLARD, M. (ed.) (1970) *New Movements in the Study and Teaching of History* (London, Temple Smith).

BARNES, D. (1969) *Language, the Learner and the School* (Harmondsworth, Penguin).

BELL, K. (1964) 'The Logical Thinking of Children in Primary Schools when Learning History' (M.Ed., Reading).

BERNBAUM, G. (1972) 'Language and History Teaching', in Burston and Green (1972), pp. 39-50.

BERNSTEIN, B. (1965) 'A Socio-Linguistic Approach to Social Learning', in J. Gould (ed.), *Social Science Survey* (Harmondsworth, Penguin).

BLYTH, W.A.L. *et al.* (1972) *An Interim Statement* (London Schools Council).

——(1973) *Spotlights: A Summary of the Project's Approach* (London, Schools Council History, Geography and Social Science Project 8-13).

BRUNER, J.S. (1963) *The Process of Education* (Cambridge, Mass., Harvard).

——(1966) *Towards a Theory of Instruction* (Cambridge, Mass., Harvard).

BRYANT, Margaret E. (1970) 'Documentary and Study Materials for Teachers and Pupils', in *Teaching History,* vol. 1, no. 3, pp. 194-202; vol. 2, no. 4, pp. 272-8.

——(1971) 'Documentary and Study Materials for Teachers and Pupils', in *Teaching History,* vol. 2, no. 5, pp. 35-47.

BURSTON, W.H. and GREEN, C.W. (eds.) (1972) *Handbook for History Teachers* (London, Methuen, rev. edn).

BURSTON W.H. and THOMPSON, D. (1967) *Studies in the Nature and Teaching of History* (London, Routledge).

COLTHAM, J. (1960) 'Junior School Children's Understanding of Some Terms Commonly Used in the Teaching of History' (Ph.D., Manchester).

——(1971) *The Development of Thinking and the Learning of History* (London, Historical Association).

ELKINS, K. and PORTER, M. (1967) *Classroom Research on Subgroup Experiences in a U.S. History Class* (Social Sciences Education Consortium, Colorado).

FREEMAN, J. (1969) *Team Teaching in Britain* (London, Ward Lock).

HALLAM, R.N. (1967) 'Logical Thinking in History', in *Educational Review,* vol. 19, no. 3, pp. 183-202.

——(1969) 'Piaget and the Teaching of History', in *Educational Research,* vol. 12, no. 1, pp. 3-12.

——(1970) 'Piaget and Thinking in History', in Ballard (1970), pp. 162-78.

HANNAM, C.L. (1969) 'Projects and Group Work', in *Teaching History,* vol. 1, no. 2, pp. 72-5.

JAHODA, G.H. (1963) 'Children's Concepts of Time and History', in *Educational Review,* vol. 15, no. 2, pp. 87-104.

KAYE, B. and ROGERS, R. (1968) *Group Work in Secondary Schools* (London, OUP).

KELLY, A. (1974) *Teaching Mixed Ability Classes* (New York, Harper & Row).

LAWTON, D. (1968) *Social Class, Language and Education* (London, Routledge).

PEEL, E.A. (1960) *The Pupil's Thinking* (London, Oldbourne).

＿＿ (1967) 'Some Problems in the Psychology of History Teaching', in Burston and Thompson (1967), pp. 159-90.

RICHARDSON, Elizabeth (1973) *The Environment of Learning* (London, Heinemann).

STEEL, D.J. and TAYLOR, L. (1973) *Family History in Schools* (Chichester, Phillimore).

STONES, S.K. (1967) 'Factors Influencing the Capacity of Adolescents to Think in Abstract Terms in the Understanding of History' (M.Ed., Manchester).

TABA, H. (1962) *Curriculum Development: Theory and Practice* (New York, Harcourt, Brace & World Inc.).

＿＿ (1969-71) *Taba Social Studies Curriculum: Teachers' Guides,* vols. 1-8 (New York, Addison Wesley).

＿＿ *et al.* (1971) *A Teacher's Handbook to Elementary Social Studies: An Inductive Approach* (New York, Addison Wesley).

THOMAS, J.B. (1971) 'Group Teaching in Advanced Level History', in *Teaching History* vol. 2, no. 5, pp. 66-9.

THOMPSON, D. (1972) 'Some Psychological Aspects of History Teaching' in Burston and Green (1972) pp. 13-38.

WARWICK, D. (1971) *Team Teaching* (London, ULP).

WATTS, D.G. (1972) *Learning of History* (London, Routledge).

Practice

EDUCATIONAL DEVELOPMENT CENTRE (1970) *Man: A Course of Study* (Washington, Curriculum Development Associates).

FAIRLEY, J. (1967) *Patch History and Creativity* (Harlow, Longmans).

FERGUSON, S. (1968) *Projects in History* (Harlow, Longmans).

＿＿ (1970) 'The Project Method', in Ballard (1970) pp. 179-91.

GENERAL STUDIES PROJECT (1969) *Using a Set* (London, Schools Council).

JAMIESON, A. (1971) *Practical History Teaching* (London, Evans).

JONES, R.B. (ed.) (1973) *Practical Approaches to the New History* (London, Hutchinson).

LAMONT, W. (1970) 'The Uses and Abuses of Examinations', in Ballard (1970), pp. 192-204.

MAYS, Pamela (1974), *Why Teach History?* (London ULP).

MILNE, A. (1973) 'Project Work at O-Level', in Jones (1973) pp. 133-60.

MORAY HOUSE PUBLICATIONS (1965) no. 2: *History in the Primary School* (Edinburgh, Moray House).

POLLARD, M. (1973) *History with Juniors* (London, Evans).

RANCE, P. (1968) *Teaching by Topics* (London, Ward Lock).

SOUTHERN REGIONAL EXAMINATIONS BOARD (n.d.) *The Assessment of Project Work,* Paper 8.

Chapter 4

Examinations in History:

their role in assessment

It seems likely, however, that teachers of history, as of any other subject, having made a large investment of time and energy, having developed a commitment to a particular syllabus or a set of syllabuses are unwilling or unable, in effect, to write off the value of that investment. Complain about examining boards, yes; seek the removal of minor irritations and constraints certainly; but strike out along new and unknown paths where previous experience may become irrelevant — this may be too much to ask of anyone, whether teacher or not.

> B.J. Holley (1974) *A-Level Syllabus Studies: History and Physic* (London, Macmillan), p. 21.

Hence the paradox: in reacting against the 'academic' aridities of the conventional examination papers many of the C.S.E. papers moved closer to the academic criteria of the professional historian.

> W. Lamont 'The Uses and Abuses of Examinations', in M. Ballard (ed.) (1970) *New Movements in the Study and Teaching of Histor* (London, Temple-Smith), p. 202.

History examinations are an endless and fascinating paradox. On the one side they have evoked perhaps the most violent criticism of any aspect in history teaching from both pupils and teacher. Every article on history examinations, in the last five years, whether at 'O' or 'A' level, has been inspired by their failings. There has also been a rising tide and a growing welcome for new approaches so that, to recall Lamont's words: 'the conventional examination papers in history now face their sternest challenge' (1970: 203). Yet, by the simple criterion of statistics, history is still a very popular subject. In 1969 3 per cent of all candidates for university admission had history as their first choice — the Bronze Medal in the Humanities League![1] — while 'O' level and CSE were not far behind.

Of course no aspect of education has been more continuously debated than the role of examinations; history is in no way unique in the sharpness of its present controversies. The first of these is, as Lamont has pointed out, that 'if history does not repeat itself, examination papers in history do' (1970: 192). In other words the timed essay-style paper is still expected to test all the skills, subject values and understanding which history teaching strives to develop. Criticism of its failure to do this is becoming more frequent even from 'A' level teachers like Dawson and Jones (1973), but the interesting point is that this debate was raised just as sharply by Happold in 1928; 'Is our history teaching to be reduced to filling our pupils with a mass of facts which on a certain day they must "know"? Might we not be better employed in teaching them to "find out" — to search out references quickly and accurately, to co-ordinate the results and to set them down in clear and vivid form?' But Happold was voted down then and, to judge from Holley's conclusion above, his contemporary counterparts would meet the same fate.

The lay view of public examinations also reinforces satisfaction with the *status quo*. Parents, pupils and employers all bring pressure on the school to regard examinations simply as qualifications. This has even affected secondary modern education for, following the switch to a single subject 'O' level structure after 1950, the number of candidates went up from about 3,000 in 1953 to around 20,000 in 1958. If the aim of the comprehensive school of the 1960s was to achieve greater equality of educational opportunity, one widespread interpretation of this has been to try to create more opportunities for more pupils to take more examinations — the public examination has almost become a major instrument of social justice. Society is dominated by examination fever and, contrary to the mood of the early sixties, public examinations seem more secure than ever.

Clearly the issue is not whether there should or should not be examinations — but rather what *sort* of examination is it to be?

NATIONAL EXAMINATIONS: ADVANTAGES AND DISADVANTAGES

What are the advantages and weaknesses of a national system of external examinations? These are continually rehearsed but must form a background to any consideration of subject examination development or reform in order to test the validity of their claims.

Advocates for the system will emphasise first that the teacher does not have to assume the role of both tutor and examiner and that, as a result, assessment is less 'subjective'. Next, that the rapport between teacher and pupil is not influenced by the ultimate prospect of the teacher having to act as the assessor. Lastly, they argue that regional and national standards can be more easily maintained because the examiner is moderating across a wider sample and also because it is impossible for any candidate to introduce work other than his own. In other words the procedure ensures a 'reliable' examination.

The critics begin by doubting whether an essay-type paper can ever do real justice to the abilities of an examinee or his work over the period of preparation. Secondly, they emphasise that marking at 'O' level is strongly influenced by the 'penny points system' which concentrates upon 'facts', while at 'A' level the marking of an open-ended essay question is known to involve a significant element of subjective judgement. Both of these criticisms question the 'validity' of the system. Furthermore, teachers often claim that they have little chance to influence the examinations or the system – although by law they have a right to do so, and all examination reports from 1917 onwards have emphasised that the examination is intended to follow the teaching rather than dictate the syllabus. The image becomes one of tyrant boards and oppressed teachers and pupils – a third aspect to be borne in mind.

EXAMINATIONS AND ASSESSMENT: PROBLEMS

Is not the aim of any examination to act as a terminal assessment of what a pupil has learned in a specific area and over a given period? Yet, as has already been pointed out, to be 'valid' any such examination in history has to cover a variety of skills, subject values, knowledge and understanding. The immediate issue is how far an examination system based on the timed essay-style paper can achieve these ends?

It is perhaps logical to begin at the 'eighteen plus', because there pupil and teacher motivation and development are surely at their best. At this level the questions are certainly open-ended, to judge by the number beginning 'compare', 'contrast', 'discuss'. However, as Dawson points out, they are sophisticated in form – being essentially similar to those on degree papers – and he wonders just how 'suitable' such questions are for the sixth former: 'If the open-ended essay is ideal as a vehicle for displaying academic excellence, it is nevertheless a very imprecise form of measuring attainment. Thus the examination becomes little more than a cold stew pot of yesterday's *idées reçues* in which the teacher is as much examined as the candidate' (1973: 199).

This leads on to the way in which teaching for the 'A' level is constrained by the syllabus: a *subject* rather than a student-centred examination. If Dawson's advocacy of a more skill-based approach would find support amongst the teachers in Holley's survey, the importance of 'the result' means that practice shows the reverse.

The question is, therefore, who is at fault? Do teachers feel that their ability to participate in the design and control of the examination is too limited to ensure greater 'validity'? First of all, it is a simple matter of fact that teachers are involved not only in the syllabus committees, but also form the great majority of examiners. Secondly, there can be no real complaint that board syllabuses have failed to reflect contemporary awareness of the need for variety in both range of selection and the aspects of history to be treated. The JMB, for example, now has thirty-three alternatives at this level, where the constitutional main stream has been broadened to encourage the teaching of social, economic and cultural history, while the national focus has been extended both to the twentieth century and to a global perspective.

Indeed the evidence of the recent Schools Council's survey (1974) would argue that the fault lies rather with the teachers; in the sample most confined themselves to the hardy perennials of the sixteenth, seventeenth and nineteenth centuries while only seven out of fifty-six took advantage of 'aspect' papers.[2] As the opening quotation suggested, teachers in the sample did not appear to be seeking any fundamental or radical change.

The issue is the importance placed on 'reliability'. Since so much is at stake in the result, can teachers be blamed for conservatism? As Dawson goes on to say. 'little research has been done on the efficiency of existing types of question, and "A" level papers are not pre-tested to eliminate those questions that mislead candidates. The Boards could have done more. They could have been better supported by the Schools Council; but because of the nature of 'A' level as a qualifying examination for university selection, experiments have been at a minimum' (1973: 205).

At 'O' level, however, there is more agreement on the need for reform and the line-up of critics is formidable: Thompson, Jones, Roberts and Macintosh to cite only a few. (The strength of feeling is perhaps best exemplified by the fact that some academically-orientated schools simply by-pass the examination for fear of alienating their pupils.) In the *Handbook for History Teachers* (1972) two Examiners offer their analysis of aims at this level: 'all the questions are — or should be — unambiguous, and in most instances there is only one answer. The majority of questions are concerned with historical events, and a typical answer consists of short descriptions or explanations of selected events. It is the answer the Chief Examiner expected because, if the question has been properly worded, it is the only possible answer' (1972: 175).

Again it is an argument based on the need for 'reliability'. However, as Roberts (1973) points out, there is no given explanation or accepted interpretation of questions like 'How did Stalin serve Russia?' He goes on to quote a variety of examples from recent papers in his syllabus — the popular European History 1871-1955. He concludes that such an attitude to assessment 'may have been acceptable in the 1890s when history was believed to be scientific' but 'when I first read the Gasson/Stokes chapter, I thought it might be a parody!' As Thompson noted, such an influence carries other dangers: 'there is considerable evidence to suggest that the way history is often taught sacrifices the development of the pupil's historical understanding to the accumulation of largely inert information and that this persists into the Sixth Form' (1972: 34). Both of these criticisms question the 'validity' of the examination and here it is noticeable that in recent years both teachers and Boards have initiated reforms, as the articles by Milne and Roberts and the example from the Associated Examining Board (see below, p. 77) shows.

DEVELOPMENTS FROM CSE

Teachers are now seeing the CSE as an alternative to the 'O' level. However, it is important to realise that the desire for an alternative originated in the need to develop a more generally acceptable form of the local leaving certificate. The main importance of CSE has been twofold: first, the development of assessment techniques more closely geared to the needs of this age group; secondly, promoting teacher involvement — even the CSE Mode I, externally set and moderated, was developed on a regional basis, while the Mode III invited individual schools or teachers to submit their own syllabuses and assessments.

These innovations coincided with the rapid expansion of interest in curriculum reform and with the foundation of the Schools Council, a major aspect of whose early work lay in this field. There is no doubt that this national support secured the more general acceptance of what was a fairly radical innovation and if Mode I has always been the largest numerically, Modes II and III are now accepted alternatives. In addition, CSE Grade I is now accepted as equivalent to the 'O' level pass and the 1971 figures, for instance, show 69,000 CSE candidates as against 62,000 for the 'O' level.[3]

As Lamont has pointed out, developments in CSE have now tended to become a model for developments in examining in history as a whole. Obviously the freedom offered by Mode III has encouraged some extremely well conceived schemes. These have not only been in the form of new syllabuses but also in the ways in which new forms of assessment have been developed to supplement the traditional three-hour paper. The inclusion of a 'project' in the examination was originally developed at this level. The second innovation has been the development of objective testing, while the third shift has been towards the inclusion of more course assessment.

But as one Board Secretary has argued, the problems of CSE can be almost the reverse of those of 'O' level. By law, the Regional Boards have to accept the syllabuses presented to them and can only suggest that the aims, content and assessment are not sufficiently taxing to be worth more than a low grade, so that if the full range of grades is to be within the candidate's grasp, the syllabus will need to be revised! In extreme cases, therefore, the teacher-centred philosophy can mean that standards of validity and reliability are equally threatened.

TOWARDS A NEW FORM OF EXAMINATION

What is becoming clear across all the levels of school examinations in history is the need for more agreement on criteria of validity and tests of reliability. Of course there are ways in which examiners and teachers are already restyling examinations. The 'project' is now being adopted at 'O' level (Milne: 1973) and is already used for the 'A' level by the Cambridge Board. This is leading teachers and examiners on to analyse much more carefully their criteria of judgement for such work. At the same time objective testing has now become much more widespread and more sophisticated, as in multiple-choice questions based on the interpretation of evidence and visuals.[4] The other development, perhaps through a backwash effect, has been the realisation that far too much attention has been concentrated on the gallop towards some terminal examination — that a more 'valid' form of course assessment might be given by a pupil 'profile' based on the complete course.

(1) *The AEB example*
The Associated Examining Board 'O' level in social and economic history affords a good example of combining such techniques. It employs three stages: a multiple-choice objective test designed not only to examine knowledge of specific facts but of relationships such as cause and effect, and to discriminate between conflicting interpretations. The second paper is based upon sets of stimulus material, aimed at testing a candidate's ability to identify relevant material, to criticise arguments in terms of their consistency and to interpret numerical data such as statistics. The final paper can then use the essay question, in a genuinely open-ended manner, to test the candidate's ability not only to draw upon evidence and to develop coherent argument and narrative, but to enter 'imaginatively' into the past. This move towards a varied form of assessment now appears to have secured recognition by almost all the Boards. In 1974, for example, the London Board changed its most popular 'O' level syllabus from an examination based on a single essay-type paper to one mirroring the above approach.

(2) *The basic issues*
The essential problem, however, is that though examination boards frequently offer detailed guidance on content, only exceptionally do they articulate explicit teaching aims and objectives. This is clearly demonstrated in the Gasson and Stokes article (1972). They state that

for any Mode III submission 'there should be a preamble to the details of the scheme which sets out clearly the aims and objectives of the scheme (i.e. what skills are to be developed; what subject-matter is considered relevant for these pupils; what attitudes of thought it is hoped will be nurtured by following this scheme)' (1972: 183-4). However, while they show how to expand an outline syllabus, they give no further guidance on how to specify the more difficult areas of skills, relevance and teaching approach. This is the weakness which Henry Macintosh has underscored in his three questions (and the echo of Roy Wake's questions on selection should not be missed):

1. What do we want to do?
2. How can we achieve what we want to do?
3. How can we assess whether we have achieved what we want to do?
(1973: 193)

CONCLUSION

Developing such sophisticated forms of valid and reliable assessment, however, demands a great deal, both of the examination board as designers and from the teacher operating the new techniques. As the CSE Mode III has highlighted, these techniques carry the always unwelcome prospect of increased work load and personal responsibility. Not unnaturally this changing situation, and the increased demands on their time, are making many teachers feel insecure and it is small comfort to be told that this is paralleled by uncertainty at the Boards.

The important conclusion, however, is that innovation in this field is calling for the signing of a new contract on the whole role and status of examinations. Can we hope to assess the skills, abilities and under-standings in much greater detail than before unless we discuss what are the skills and concepts that might be achieved at each age/ability level? In other words does not an involvement in 'improving examinations' in history have direct implications for encouraging greater professional participation in history teaching as a whole?

NOTES

1. UCCA 7th Report, Table 2, cited in R.B. Jones 'Towards a New History Syllabus', in *History*, vol. 55, no. 185 (1970) p. 384.
2. The selected aspect papers were America 3, Social and Economic 2, and Special Topic: Age of Discovery, 1. Henry VIII, 1.
3. Cited in HMSO, *Abstract of Educational Statistics* (1971).
4. See the Methuen series 'Handbooks on Objective Testing'.

BIBLIOGRAPHY

ASTLEY, I.D. (1969) 'Some Recent Trends in CSE History' in *Teaching History*, vol. 1, no. 1, pp. 12-18.

BALLARD, M. (ed.) (1970) *New Movements in the Study and Teaching of History* (London, Temple Smith).

BRAGDON, H.W. (1968) 'History Tests: Uses and Abuses', in J.S. Roucek, *The Teaching of History* (London, Peter Owen), pp. 233-45.

BRUCE, G. (1969) *Secondary School Examinations* (Oxford, Pergamon).

BURSTON, W.H. and GREEN, C.W. (eds.) (1972) *Handbook for History Teachers* (London, Methuen, rev. edn).

CAPES, R.G. (1970) 'Mode 3 CSE' in *Trends in Education*, no. 20, pp. 16-20.

DAWSON, K. and JONES, R.B. (1973) 'History and the 18+', in Jones (1973), pp. 196-225.

DOCKING, J.W. (1970) 'History and the CSE', in *Teaching History*, vol. 1, no. 4, pp. 292-6.

EGGLESTON, J. and HOLFORD, D. (1971) 'Recent Trends in Examining, Parts I and II', in *Forum*, vol. 13, no. 2, pp. 40-4 and vol. 14, no. 1, pp. 20-6.

GARRETT, S. and WATSON, J.B. (1973) 'World History – the Curriculum and its Assessment', in *Teaching History*, vol. 3, no. 10, pp. 137-42.

GASSON, P.C. and STOKES, W.P. (1972) 'The GCE Ordinary Level and the CSE Examinations', in Burston and Green (1972), pp. 173-86.

HAPPOLD, F. (1928) *The Approach to History* (Christophers).

HARTOG, P.J. and RHODES, E.C. (1935) *An Examination of Examinations* (New York, Columbia).

HOLLEY, B.J. (1974) *A-Level Syllabus Studies: History and Physics* (London, Macmillan).

IAAM (1966) *The Teaching of History in Secondary Schools* (Cambridge, CUP), pp. 103-17.

JOINT MATRICULATION BOARD (1964) *The Marking of Scripts in Advanced Level History* (Manchester, JMB).

JONES, R.B. (1972) 'Oakham School Mode III History O-Level', in *Teaching History*, vol. 2, no. 7, pp. 269-72.

____ (ed.) (1973) *Practical Approaches to the New History* (London, Hutchinson).

LAMONT, W. (1970) 'The Uses and Abuses of Examinations', in Ballard (1970), pp.192-204.

LAWTON, D. and DUFOUR, B. (1973) *The New Social Studies: A Handbook for Teachers in Primary, Secondary and Further Education*, Part V: 'Evaluation', pp. 367-463 (London, Heinemann).

MACINTOSH, H.G. (1971) 'Assessment in O-Level History' in *Teaching History*, vol. 2, no. 5, pp. 53-7.

____ (1973) 'Assessment at Sixteen-Plus in History', in Jones (1973) pp. 161-95.

MACINTOSH, H.G. and QUINN, J.Q. (1971), *Economic and Social History: Objective Testing Series* (London, Methuen).

—— (1972) *European History 1789-1945: Objective Testing Series*, (London, Methuen).

MILNE, A. (1973) 'Project Work at O-Level: A Review of a Recent Pilot Scheme', in Jones (1973), pp. 132-60.

PEARCE, J. (1972) *School Examinations* (New York, Collier-Macmillan).

ROBERTS, M. (1973) 'A Different Approach to O-Level', in Jones (1973) pp. 109-31.

RUST, B.R. (1973) *Objective Testing in Education and Training* (London, Pitman).

SCHOOLS COUNCIL (1968) *The Certificate of Secondary Education: The Place of the Personal Topic − History* (London, HMSO).

THOMPSON, D. (1972) 'Some Psychological Aspects of History Teaching' in Burston and Green (1972), pp. 13-38.

WATSON, J.B. (1970) 'A-Level without Recriminations' in *Teaching History*, vol. 1, no. 4, pp. 297-9.

Chapter 5

Evidence and Enquiry:

the role of resources

> The most austere [teacher] is likely to employ a blackboard and
> books. To these some teachers now add, from time to time,
> broadcasts, records, slides, film-loops, overhead projector
> transparencies, films. Indeed, the modern teacher, as he emerges
> in conferences and in articles, is expected to achieve prodigies of
> co-ordination, busking his restive audience like a one-man band.
>
> L.C. Taylor (1971) *Resources for Learning* (Harmondsworth,
> Pelican), p. 178.

> To discuss resources is to ask questions about educational aims,
> objectives, methods and outcomes.
>
> J. Hanson (1975), *The Use of Resources* (London, Allen &
> · Unwin), p. 12.

To 'learn how to learn', to 'communicate the mode of enquiry of the
specialist', do not the 'Brunerian articles' form the basis of our
contemporary creed? History is peculiarly suited to such an approach;
it may be about the past but it is a human past and its texture is rich
in sight, sound, touch and smell. Yet every teacher who has embraced
this faith has surely found that interest has ranged far wider than the
textbook or even the resources of the library and, as consultant, he has
been worn ragged by the endless questions and demands for more from
the classroom Olivers!

Until recently the lack of suitable materials has been the main
difficulty in developing enquiry and evidential approaches — a point
endorsed by the emphasis on 'materials production' in the briefs of
almost all the 'first generation' curriculum development projects. Yet,
in the short space of about five years, the reverse has become true.
Schools Council and Nuffield materials have almost been swamped by
colourful commercial packages. Then, as John Hanson has said, 'all
the world's a resource', and teachers have shown tremendous ingenuity
in the ways in which they have exploited this store. Yet has it all been
to good purpose? If 'good' means encouraging or reviving interest —
then 'yes', undoubtedly so. But if 'good' means 'learning how to learn'
and initiation into the 'mode of enquiry', then the judgement must be
more qualified.

BASIC CONSIDERATIONS

(1) *The criteria for selection*

Resources are for learning – Taylor (1971) put this so well, his title alone is the message. His answer was that resources alone were not enough, it was 'packages' not 'programmes' that were needed and the teachers were the essential mediators. John Hanson follows this through in his *Use of Resources,* where the core chapter is entitled 'Criteria for Selecting and Designing Resources'.[1] He begins by making the distinction between the mode of enquiry, or of finding out; and the mode of experience, of 'understanding and expression'. For these he distinguishes six contributing elements: those of motivation, instruction, search, problem-solving, concept-formation and presentation. His analysis is very clear; the terms are well chosen and so much part of current language that they surely do not need elaboration. They offer criteria to be applied across all the 'tools' that history teachers use.

(2) *Application to learning activities*

A parallel consideration is the application of these criteria within the differing circumstances of teacher-led, pupil-centred or resource-based learning activities. A teacher, even as 'consultant' or 'neutral chairman' has to select, to inspire interest in his choice, to explain (or stimulate questions by probing) – in short he is the *strategist,* the guide and the monitor of standards. Here resources help; they can develop interest, instruct or explain, raise questions or set exercises for tests. In sum they help to take the *operational* burden off the teacher. Pupil-centred activities in guides for search or problem-solving relate teacher and resources. Their other aim is to put the focus on the learner. The issue is tactical; does the balance encourage individual initiative or constrain it within a defined or common frame? The medium is important but is only partly the message because education is primarily aimed at the development of the pupil.

(3) *Practical problems*

Practical considerations are also essential. First, *time* – for thought, discussion and preparation: 'the major obstacle to any change . . . is the time it takes to produce, collect or arrange' (Taylor, 1971: 8). Then *media:* if books have been, and perhaps must always remain, the stock in trade of history teachers – how can a slide, tape or film enhance this context? Are they supplementary, complementary or do they introduce new possibilities for learning? Next, *cost:* the ever-present bogey! Not only does a school have to possess the soft and hard-ware, but optimally the teacher ought to be able to encourage his pupils to use these creatively: to take photographs, to make recordings or even films, and then to communicate their findings or interpretations to their peers.

(4) *Conclusion*

The English tradition stresses respect for the autonomy of the teacher and, in the present situation, he has three choices: first, to find a published scheme which covers his personal, or the school's aims. Does this seem likely? It is certainly the easiest thing to do! The opposite is to design all his own materials, because those available either do not tackle the issue in the way he would like or are not suitable for the needs of his particular pupils. In the present situation this is probably unrealistic. The most usual development is that of a *mix* of systems and media, where published materials supplement a framework or a published scheme is enriched by the addition of local resources. These then are the needs, and the rest of the chapter examines the resources that the history teacher has at his disposal and suggests ways in which he can assess both their value for history and their suitability for his pupils.

BOOKS

(1) *General outlines*

Books are still the staple for history teaching. If the 'traditional' textbook is now mostly relegated to a back shelf, the widening range of syllabuses has encouraged a proliferation of outline surveys — such as the Penguin and Longmans series. At the same time the accent on study in depth has stimulated an ever-increasing flow of 'topic' or 'evidential' studies — such as the ubiquitous 'Then and There' (Longmans) and the sixth-form 'World Studies Series' (Routledge).

Taking the first of these categories: what have been and usually still are its main functions? Conventionally it has been the main source of narrative explanation, information and reference. However, cannot these criteria be examined more specifically?

What historical values does the book express?
Does its narrative show concern for the human and particular?
Does its explanation convey that history is essentially based on evidence and so upon interpretation and judgement?
How does it represent all the four levels of historical concept outlined in Chapter 3?

Does it encourage an enquiry approach?
Is it usefully organised for reference?
What use does it make of the visual: maps, graphs or pictures?
Does it use the latter as hard evidence or simply for decoration?
Does it encourage further enquiry beyond its own covers?

What is its range of suitability?
How complex is its use of language?
What emphasis is there upon the special vocabulary of history?
How does it use and explain generalisation?

All these are surely essential questions for the teacher to consider when making his choice amongst the variety available to him. Rarely, however, does he have the time to do this and here the schedule (Chart 11) offers a suggestion for a quick check list. In the experience of the group of teachers who developed it, the list greatly facilitated effective sampling.

Chart 11 A BOOK ASSESSMENT SCHEDULE

| AUTHOR | TYPE | no. of pages | index |
| TITLE | LEVEL | dimensions | glossary / bibliography |

A	Simplicity ... Complexity / Precise ... Vague / Flow ... Staccato	F	Personalised ... Generalised	
		G	Explicit ... Implicit / Concrete e.g. ... Abstract ideas	
B	0-1 1-3 3-5 / Well explained ... Not explained	H	Argued ... Given	
C	Concrete ... Generalisation	I	O Y C P / Structuring by children ... Given	
D	Active ... Passive			
E	Particular and detailed ... Generalised / Qualified moral judgement ... Unsupported or absent	J	Contemporary ... Imaginative / Complimentary ... Decorative / Near ... Distant	
		K	Provided ... Not provided	
L	: Good / / / / / Poor			

Guide to Schedule

A — Use of language
B — Special terminology
C — Facts
D — Treatment of facts
E — Concern for human beings
F — Views of society
G — Notion of change
H — Cause-effect
I — Time
J — Illustrations
K — Activities and exercises suggested
L — Format

Source: J. Coltham (1970) 'Assessing History Books', in *Teaching History*, vol. 1, no. 3, p. 214.

(2) *Topic books*
The kinds of questions aspect studies raise are most of those above but also perhaps:

For the values of history
How full a background do they create for their study — are they self-sufficient or supportive?
What are the range of evidences that they draw upon?
How do they illustrate and encourage interpretation through comparison or contrast?
What degree of 'imaginative involvement' might result from either the documentary or visual material?

For enquiry
What skills of search do they develop?
How do they develop opportunities for 'problem-solving'?
What further enquiries do they actively encourage?

For suitability
How far can such books be envisaged as being used independently by pupils?
If so, do they need, or include, any self-testing procedures?

KITS

A more novel field of development, resulting from the drive to motivate and extend evidential approaches, has been the development of kits. The obvious attraction is that they offer greater flexibility, both for enquiry and in style of presentation. They range from the simple work card collections such as Ladybird or Wayland, through the 'aspect' compilations such as Jackdaw or archive, to the 'patch' syllabuses such as the BBC 'History in Evidence' and the Macmillan series. The main questions these raise are broadly the same as those listed under books but it is worth highlighting others:

For historical value
How does the compilation exploit the possibility of presenting a greater range of evidences than the book? (especially in media)

For enquiry
What kind of 'path', either implicit or explicit, does it suggest?
How far does it facilitate individual or small group learning?
(this is often indicated simply by the number of copies of materials!)

For suitability
How easy is it to handle — first, for the pupils, and second, in terms of durability and storage?

Another useful checklist for archives by Hallward is reproduced in Chart 12.

Chart 12 AN ARCHIVE AND KIT ASSESSMENT SCHEDULE

Section I: **General**

Title	. . . .	Author	. . . .
Producer	. . . .	Publisher	. . . .
Type	. . . .	Cost	. . . .
Index	. . . .	Bibliography	. . . .
Glossary	. . . .	Related Audio-Visual Material	. . .
Age Range	. . . .	Ability Range	. . . .

Section II: **Format**

	No	Size	Quality	Language
Container				
Documents				
Maps				
Charts				
Photographs				
Illustrations				
Assignment Cards				
Information (teacher)				
Information (pupil)				

Section III: **Questions and Activities**

A: Comprehension Multiple Choice/True-False Tabulating Research (Find out)	C: Involve other Disciplines Involve Particular Skills (e.g. transcription, translation, palaeography)
B: Imaginative Writing Drawing Model Making Drama Visits	D: Then/Now Comparisons Discussion/Opinion Children to Pose Questions Evaluation (e.g. Why was it made? Of what event did it form part? What form is it in? How reliable is it? What is the overall message or meaning of the document) E: Other

Source: Christabell Hallward (1973) 'Archive Units and History Kits: An Evaluation', in *History in School*, no. 1 (Leeds University), p. 8.

GAMES AND SIMULATIONS

A logical development from the evidential approach has been the
attempt either to simulate an historical event or to re-create the past
through a game. Originally American, this approach has recently
become very popular, and is associated with the names of Pat Tansey
(1971) and Rex Walford (1969).

A simulation attempts to re-create a particular situation in order to
explore why an event or situation tended to follow the path it did. Its
focus is therefore on role-playing and decision-making. For younger
pupils it has mainly been employed in social or moral education, as for
example the Lifeline series: 'In Other People's Shoes' (Longmans, 1972).
In history, the need to understand the human and situational complexities has meant that it has tended to be used more at an adult level, as
the well-known 'Middle East Crisis' illustrates.

The aim of a game is to explain an historical concept such as 'trade'
or 'enclosure'. The attraction for the pupil is the basic stimulus of
competition and what the teacher needs to examine is how far he can
set the game in a learning context through preparation, additional
examples and comparative explanation. The early but now classic
example is Walford's 'The Railway Pioneers' (1969, 64-76) which
deals with the opening up of the Western USA by the railroads after
1860. As any historian knows, this was a highly competitive situation
so there is a real need to set the game in the context of the historical,
geographic and economic problems involved and the way in which
human resource and technology were used to overcome them. Tackled
in this way the competitive aspect of the game can be utilised as a
stimulus to further enquiry; otherwise experience has shown that the
result tends only to reinforce nascent capitalistic values which could
equally well be gained in 'Monopoly'! (A very good series of these
games, all of which have been tested in schools, is now being provided
by the Longmans Resources Unit.)

ARTEFACTS

Knowledge of the past, and so our attempt to re-create it, is essentially
experiential. As Margaret Bryant has said, it is the sights, sounds and
smells which provide both the attraction and the texture of the past.
Museums and their schools services have been making imaginative
efforts to meet this need, as in the 'story of boats' in the Neptune
Room of the Maritime Museum or the 'Please Touch' exhibition at the
American Museum at Bath. The material is there, though often
severely overworked, as the Tutankhamen exhibition proved. At the
same time teachers are realising what rich sources of evidence they
possess in the street, the churchyard, the workplace and local tradition.

The main questions here seem to be:

For history
What skills, values and attitudes are being encouraged here?
How far does either viewing research, as in archaeology at Danebury, or reconstruction, as in the Geffrye museum, help towards the goal of empathy?

For enquiry and suitability
What links are being developed between the evidence and some enquiry (and how explicitly are these being brought to the pupils' attention)? What are the differences between such visits and examining artefacts in the classroom? (One is the well-known problem of the 'cattle-drive' with its ever-present danger of 'stampede' and endless need for 'round-up' (!) against the careful and tangible examination of a selected number of pieces.)

VISUAL AND AURAL MATERIAL

(1) *Wallcharts*
Visual sources have been greatly enlarged recently, but have always been available to the teacher. Consider first the well-known wall chart:

What are its historical values?
Does it demonstrate a perspective or inter-relationship clearly?
Is this too simplistic an analysis in relationship to current interpretations?

In terms of presentation
Is the language and terminology suitable?
Has it been well designed? (Contrast for example two recent time-charts on China: the colourful but muddling Jackdaw with the clear but more austere *Sunday Times* example.)

(2) *Stills, slides and filmstrips*
The picture is rapidly becoming much more widely used in the class-room, and the traditional 'composite' is seen less often as the evidential approach argues for actuality. Excellent examples are to be found in the 'Focus on History Series' where the illustrations are either photographic or contemporary.

For history
Is the picture being used purely decoratively or as evidence?
If the latter, then what percepts are the pupils supposed to gain?

In suitability
How important is size, particularly for details (are the pictures large

enough for class groups as in MACOS, or provided in class sets as in the Humanities Curriculum Project)?
If the latter, do they need to be supported by carefully thought out notes and questions so that these can be used flexibly either by individuals or small groups.

The advantage of the projected picture lies in its size; its weakness is the need for 'blackout' — an elementary but often deficient requirement. However, the range of available slides and filmstrips is now so wide that greater use of some selective criteria is badly needed: so many are bought on impulse and just rattle around unused. (Even the well produced Historical Association packs only appear to be organised under the simple rationale of content. Neither the selection nor the notes lead the learner (or the teacher) to greater awareness of historical issues, or of the range of evidences that the historian uses in constructing his narrative.)

Another choice to be made is between filmstrips and slides. The advantage of the strip is argued to be a sequential presentation. However, classroom evidence suggests that this not only takes too much time but also induces passivity rather than participation in the audience.

(3) *Tape recording*

The cheap tape-recorder is now also a familiar piece of equipment so that criteria for its use are also important. Using it as *input* can help in the re-creation of the past, either in bringing oral evidence (or, for sixth formers, the voice of the historian) into the classroom. Again:

For the values of history and enquiry
Is this being examined as evidence or merely supportive in helping to create atmosphere?

In presentation
Is the language at the right level?
Are the length of the extract and the range of issues within the pupils' grasp?

The other way in which the tape-recorder can be helpful is in *output*, in bringing together pupils' discussions in order to help them either compare or re-examine their judgements critically.

(4) *Radio*

As a footnote here, it is perhaps worth adding how much teachers could gain from the current programmes now being put out by BBC radio, ranging from *Man* to *History in Evidence*. These are well supported by suggestive 'starter' work kits.

(5) *Television*

Many schools now use the carefully prepared and magnificently resourced BBC and ITV programmes. The only general complaint is of the rigidity of the schedules! Yet relevant questions are:

> *How far is the television being used:*
> To support evidential and enquiry approaches?
> As a form of evidence?
> For atmosphere?
> Simply to provide more attractive outline narrative?

(6) *Film*

The questions above are becoming real matters for debate because of the increasing use of film at all levels of history teaching — and especially for the twentieth century.[2] The British Universities Film Council have now made three experimental films mainly based on newsreel evidence; the British Film Institute offers a well chosen series of clips from famous historical films; while *Man: A Course of Study* is built around the filmed studies of two specialists in order to communicate the 'mode of enquiry' being used. In these examples, there is a progression from illustration to apparently raw data. The latter raise the further question of 'actuality': how far is the fact that film is an artefact, shot for specific purposes, an issue to be explored? At the other extreme is Tom Hastie's advocacy of feature film (1969, 1972). Here the problem is the obvious need to prepare the audience, as his notes on the Chinese Communist epic 'The Opium War' illustrate very clearly! (1969: 39-41).

CONCLUSION

The conclusions are surely simple and obvious. First, that when such rich and stimulating resources are available, the cry that history is 'in danger' could only frighten an ostrich — a bird which is not indigenous to Britain! Second that, once again, to select within such variety asks for some criteria if the judgement is to be 'objective' and helpful.

NOTES

1. Hanson's book is concerned with the criteria for the selection of resources, with the practical problems of structuring a unit of study and then choosing the optimum means for preparing it. It is designed to be complementary to all the books in this series.
2. See Pronay (1972).

BIBLIOGRAPHY

BRITISH UNIVERSITIES FILM COUNCIL (1968) *Film and the Historian,* No. 1 (London BUFC).

____ (1972) *Films for Historians* (London, BUFC).

COLTHAM, J. (1970) 'Assessing History Books', in *Teaching History,* vol. 1, no. 3, pp. 213-18.

DES (1968) *Archives and Education* (London, HMSO).

FINES, J. (1968) 'Archives in School', in *History,* vol. 53, no. 179, pp. 348-56.

HALLWARD, Christabell (1973) 'Archive Units and History Kits: An Evaluation', in *History in School,* no. 1 (Leeds University) pp. 1-8.

HANCOCK, Joy and JOHNSON Helen (1972) 'Archive Kits in Secondary Schools', in *Teaching History,* vol. 2, no. 7, pp. 207-17.

HANSON, J. (1975) *The Use of Resources* (London, Allen & Unwin).

HASTIE, T. (ed.) (1969) *Feature Films and the History Teacher* (London History Teachers Association).

MILBURN, G. (1972) 'Simulations in History Teaching: Promising Innovation or Passing Fad?', in *Teaching History,* vol. 2, no. 7, pp. 236-41.

NEWCOMBE, C. (1970) 'War Games in the Classroom', in *Teaching History,* vol. 1, no. 4, pp. 300-2.

NICHOL, J. (1972) 'Simulation and History Teaching – Trade and Discovery, a History Game for Use in Schools', in *Teaching History,* vol. 2, no. 7, pp. 242-8.

____ and BIRT, D. (1973) 'Ironmaster: A History Simulation for Use in Schools and Colleges', in *Teaching History,* vol. 3, no. 9, pp.12-25.

PRONAY, N. *et al.* (1972) *The Use of Film in History Teaching* (London, Historical Association).

SCHOOLS COUNCIL (n.d.) *Games and Simulation in the Classroom* (SC History, Geography and Social Science 8-13 Project).

TANSEY, P.J. and UNWIN, D. (1969) *Simulation and Gaming in Education* (London, Methuen).

____ (ed.) (1971) *Educational Aspects of Simulation* (New York, McGraw-Hill).

TAYLOR, J.L. and WALFORD, R. (1972) *Simulation in the Classroom* (Harmondsworth, Penguin).

TAYLOR, L.C. (1971) *Resources for Learning* (Harmondsworth, Pelican).

WALFORD, R. (1969) *Games in Geography* (Harlow, Longmans)

WALTON, J. and RUCK, J. (1975) *Resources and Resource Centres* (London, Ward Lock).

WOOD, R.G.E. (1971-3) 'Archive Units for Teaching: Parts 1, 2 and 3', in *Teaching History,* vol. 2, no. 6 (1971), pp. 158-64; vol 2, no. 7 (1972), pp. 28-35; and vol. 3, no. 9 (1973), pp. 41-5.

RESOURCE LISTS

BRITISH FILM INSTITUTE, Distribution Catalogue *(London BFI, ann.)*.

BURSTON, W.H. and GREEN, C.W. (1972) *Handbook for History Teachers* (London, Methuen). (The second part gives bibliographic lists by period, area or aspect. It can be brought up to date by relating to current reviews in the journal *History* and the *Annual Bulletin of Historical Literature,* both published by the Historical Association.)

CAMBRIDGE INSTITUTE OF EDUCATION (1967, rev. edn) *History Books* (Camb. Inst. Edn) (This gives lists of major series, historical novels, etc., with appendices on other teaching aids.)

EDUCATIONAL FOUNDATION FOR VISUAL AIDS, *Audio-Visual Aids, Part 2: History, Social History, Social Sciences* (EFVA, ann.).

INDEX PUBLISHERS, *Museums and Galleries* (London, IP, ann.).

MUSEUMS ASSOCIATION, *Museum Calendar* (London, M Assn, ann.).

OPEN UNIVERSITY FILM LIBRARY, *Catalogue* (London, OU, ann.).

SCHOOLS COUNCIL GENERAL STUDIES PROJECT, *Collections 1972-4* (York, Longmans Resources Unit).

WILLIAMS, Gwyneth (1962) *Guide to Illustrative Material for Use in Teaching History* (London, Historical Association).

____(1969) *Supplement – Transparencies* (London, Historical Association).

Chapter 6

History and Inter-Disciplinary Approaches: gain or loss?

Thus a polarity may emerge — not least among teachers — between a view of history which stresses human range and relevance, and one which stresses limitation of area and academic rigour. The first may see no need of integrated studies — history is 'the house where all subjects dwell'. The latter may regard it as a mongrel, whose bite could threaten pedigree historians.

> D. Bolam, 'History and Integrated Studies', in R.B. Jones (1973) *Practical Approaches to the New History* (London, Hutchinson), p. 256.

It is sometimes assumed that separate subject teaching creates or perpetuates an approach which is 'artificial', at least from the viewpoint of the pupil . . . It can hardly be denied that this criticism is justified to some extent by the number of dull and arbitrarily selected courses still being taught as separate subjects. Must we despair, however, of subject specialists finding ways of putting their own houses in order, as is already being attempted through new schemes of work in mathematics and science, or is there some necessity of crossing subject boundaries when reforming courses dealing with human or social material? Unfortunately this critical question has received little attention.

> C. Portal, 'The Place of History in Integrated and Interdisciplinary Studies', in W.H. Burston & C.W. Green (eds), *Handbook for History Teachers* (London, Methuen), p. 144.

'Inter-disciplinary studies' — at every level of history teaching mention of this phrase seems to provoke rising blood-pressures! Why is this so? As Marwick shows, historians have for a long time argued that, as a study, history is an 'inclusive, mediating discipline', 'the common home of many interests and techniques and traditions'.[1] Yet, in the last decade the attitude of some professional historians has usually appeared to be defensive, communicating an apparent fear of being submerged and making much of earlier criticism of attempts at broader interpretations such as Toynbee's meta-history or Weber's 'model-building'. On the other hand there are many other historians who would argue strongly that historical explanation has been both enriched and extended by making use of other disciplines. But in school teaching does not the defensive attitude still persist? History teachers appear to swing uneasily between claiming independence for the sake of the subject discipline and resisting becoming a 'service subject' within humanities and other integrated schemes — sometimes they even go so far as to aggressively assert the claim of history as the natural integrator for such an approach!

Practical explanations for this unease are obvious. Certainly part of the problem is that history has only a minority share in the general timetable (2/3 periods per week) — and in a timetable that is always becoming more overcrowded. So small changes towards 'blocking' in the humanities can result in a large effect on how much history can be taught. (But this is no different a position to that of geography or religious education in the curriculum.) More important have been the contemporary claims of the need to teach for explicit social or political education — here only specialist teachers working towards the present subject examination systems can claim independence.

The real difficulty, however, for those for and against integration, is that so much of the argument is emotional rather than logical. For many history teachers this response is the result of a lack of confidence, simply because their own training antedated most of the contemporary trends. What is forgotten, however, is that many of the advocates for integration are also guilty of purely emotional thinking — to cite only Charity James, *Young Lives at Stake.* [2] What is vitally needed is clear analysis of the rationale for integrated work and of its relation to subject teaching — a rationale which Christopher Portal (1972) argues has largely been lacking up to now. [3]

CLAIMS FOR INTEGRATED STUDIES

(1) *In the aims of education*

What are the claims of integrated studies to a place in the curriculum? First, the contemporary context cannot be ignored. Integration is being developed as a practical response to three educational aims which command very wide acceptance today. The first of these is the desire to develop a more pupil-centred education. It not only asks that the teaching shall be relevant to the pupil's capabilities, but also argues that it should stimulate his involvement through an enquiry approach — and enquiries tend not to come in simple subject packages! Deriving from this is the second aim, which is to give the pupil a clearer perception of the purposes of having a subject-based curriculum. If the pupil is to realise such a holistic view this is to argue that subjects must be 'tools' or 'resources for enquiry'. The final aim derives from society's growing social conscience and its awareness of the need to promote greater social cohesion. The claim is that an integrated approach makes it much more possible to study the 'large and complex' issues which face the contemporary world.

(2) *In the aims of the comprehensive school*
Organising for comprehensive education has seen many practical
attempts to articulate a more comprehensive curriculum embodying
these aims. Two developments have been particularly important: the
adoption of mixed-ability grouping in order to encourage social
inclusiveness and the continuing attempt to develop 'topical relevance'
in the selection of content for the curriculum. Both of these developments have had strong effects on history's place in the curriculum. The
subjects concerned with realising such social aims are obviously those
of the humanities, within which history has always been regarded as
bearing the most direct responsibility for social and political education.
Again, the adoption of the mixed ability approach has been easiest in
these subjects, as they do not appear to demand a sequential approach
to the developments of concepts and skills, and so are not organised on
a four- or five-year pattern as are mathematics, language and science
teaching.

One rider needs to be added at this point. It is that the main line of
criticism of integrated approaches has been of their failure to realise or
make specific such broad aims. For example, Burston has shown how
the term 'child-centred' has been the battledore of educational
philosophers ever since Dewey and how the appeal to 'topical relevance'
of the early sixties can be seen as very similar to the purely charismatic
appeal — and subsequent failure — of the post-1945 social studies
movement.[4] However, what he fails to discuss is how far the national,
area or school-based curriculum development projects that have appeared
since 1967 can be criticised usefully in the same general terms.

THE NATURE OF INTEGRATED STUDIES

The first point to be made is that there can be *no single form* of
integrated approach. Given the variety of original aims, the range of
practical development must be enormous. This obvious point is,
however, often overlooked both by advocates and critics. The need is,
therefore, for a critical analysis and discussion of this variety. The
model or norm here must be the conventional secondary curriculum,
of which the hallmarks are that it is subject-based and teacher-centred.
How far do the changes implied by the aims of the integrated approach
appear simply evolutionary in terms of current developments, or are
they really radical?

The aims outlined above provide convenient starting points for such
an analysis. The first surely reflects only the general contemporary
concern for the role of the learner, reflected alike in the child-centred
approach of the post-Plowden primary school, and the Goldsmiths'
Inter-Disciplinary Enquiry. The need here is to relate the interests of

the learner more closely to his 'needs' and so to distinguish between discovery and structure in enquiry.[5] The second aim introduces the problem of knowledge as a framework for the curriculum. On the one side there is the need to introduce the pupil to the disciplines as distinct 'ways of thinking', paralleled with the wish to motivate interest through 'enquiry approaches'. The emphasis on enquiry tends to imply a 'problem-solving' or 'issue-based' structure and raises the difficulty of confining such enquiries neatly within subject boundaries — this is particularly so for the humanities because of the enormous 'overlaps' involved in explanations.

Again, however, what often appears overlooked is that the results need not be radical. Good subject teaching, particularly in the humanities, has always stressed the way in which it exploits such 'bridging opportunities'. So there can be 'related' approaches which simply develop such overlaps in content through teacher co-operation. These have often led on to common syllabuses between subjects which go further in such co-ordination between content and personalities — again no novelty. The only way in which such an approach is becoming at all radical is in the growing advocacy of 'team-teaching' in such situations.

So it is the third aim, of making possible the exploration of large and complex human issues, which is the only one that demands a basic reinterpretation of why, what and how we should teach 'the study of mankind'. The problem has often been the practical one that, lacking time, too many schemes have been hastily planned. Also, teachers have not been led to appreciate how needs hang together, though any consideration of Bruner's curriculum *Man: A Course of Study* (see below, p. 100) would show just how deeply such rethinking should be approached.

In conclusion, what must be examined are the ways in which present developments in integrated studies are related to these aims. To do this properly the history teacher must be clear about his interpretation of the value of his subject and about his role in the classroom. The assumption that has been made by many is that they are bound to find a loss or 'distortion' in terms of either content or approach. Might it not, however, be of gain; in flexibility of approach, in range of content, or of working as a member of a team of specialists instead of being the 'single court of appeal'?

INTEGRATION IN THE LOWER JUNIOR SCHOOL (8-10)

Subject teaching has no obvious role here as the 'integrated day' has characterised the curriculum of the junior school since Plowden. This is, of course, determined by the close relationship between pupil and class teacher and the latter's wish to help the pupils to develop basic skills as much as knowledge at this stage. However, it is now realised that many such approaches have over-reached the capabilities of the school, not simply in terms of material resources but also of teacher understanding. The trend is now towards reconciling such 'openness' with a framework of skills and concepts for this level.

INTEGRATION IN THE MIDDLE YEARS

The curriculum conferences on the middle years of 1967 and 1973[6] both emphasised the strong arguments against too early or too abrupt a fragmentation into separate subject units. It is strongly argued that during this period of development pupils' motivation still benefits both from a close working relationship with a single teacher and from having a flexible timetable in order to allow them to follow interests or projects to some conclusion. However, the fact that this is a transitional stage, leading towards a curriculum that ultimately prepares the pupil for adult society, cannot be avoided. The result has been to argue for 'introductions' to the study of disciplines and for the beginnings of sequential approaches as refinements of earlier 'centre-of-interest' enquiries and topic-based curricula.

The history teacher is in a strong position to contribute to such an approach. It fits neatly with the trends (noticed earlier) towards introducing original sources and developing patch studies. Two very good examples are to be found in the Schools Council Integrated Studies pack *Exploration Man* (1973). The first of these is an illustration of how archaeology can contribute to understanding the living past — using the examples of the excavations and reconstructions at Danebury and Butser Hill. The second, 'Children and the War', uses the evidence of the generations — the children's families — in order to introduce them to an understanding of 'change'. In both these examples the historian is working with his subject but in a way which highlights its use as a tool of enquiry. (The six other units in *Exploration Man* each treat a different subject in this way.)

The two main areas of integration at this level are undoubtedly those of environmental and social studies. Both are of course generic titles, embracing a range of interpretations. Environmental studies, however, is generally accepted to involve learning by direct investigation of the locality, while social studies has tended to be directed towards understanding of community, whether local or national, and the place of the individual within it.

For environmental studies Watts (1967) has made the distinction between learning 'about' and 'from' the environment. He uses the latter term to describe applied specialist studies focusing upon a particular field or discipline and it is the former which he sees as the usual approach in schools. There is no doubt of its popularity, which led the Schools Council to set up its *Environmental Studies 8-13* as one of its earliest development projects. While the team survey of current work naturally discovered enormous diversity, a common factor emerged. This was the strong emphasis on the use of immediate and concrete evidence and developing the skills for treating it. Though such studies reflected a pooling of teacher expertise and the crossing of subject boundaries, their concentration was upon the skills and concepts of geography and biology — as the earlier reports and published case studies show.[7] (The same is true of the parallel development by Perry *et al.* (1971).) However, what has become generally recognised is that such approaches have often omitted the human context and the historian's contribution to developing an understanding of the way in which both past and present generations have used the environment. So the Schools Council have recently published a working paper (1973), the revised edition of Perry includes a chapter on history, and a good practical illustration is to be found in the SCISP second-level pack, *Communicating with Others,* and the churchyard and high street sections of 'Look and Listen'.

For social studies Denis Lawton's survey (1971) showed just how difficult it is to agree objectives in this field: '114 schools wrote in over 220 statements of objectives and ignoring duplications we were able to identify 140 different objectives' (1971: 148)! The main concern of this survey derived from the contemporary interest in developing social education at 14-16. Lawton felt that this aim asked for an earlier introduction to awareness of social norms, though he was aware of the difficulties of communicating many of the concepts involved. His project report suggests an interesting approach to developing a sequential curriculum to provide this base (see Chart 13). Again, as with environmental studies, the point is that the chart clearly shows a strong potential role for the history teacher.

This role has been made much more explicit in the follow-up project to Lawton's feasibility study, that of *History, Geography and the Social Sciences 8-13.* It has been exploring the ways in which the contributing subjects can be used as 'resource areas' and how teachers can help to develop more explicit understanding of their subject disciplines for their pupils. Its controversial innovation has been to explore the notion of 'key concepts'. The Project has suggested seven which it feels might be considered as common to all three disciplines: these are communication, power, values and beliefs, conflict/consensus, continuity/change, similarity/difference, causality. Parallel with the emphasis on concepts has been the project's concern to encourage teachers to define objectives in their teaching. As experience of local trials has shown,

Chart 13 **A FRAMEWORK FOR SOCIAL STUDIES 8-13**

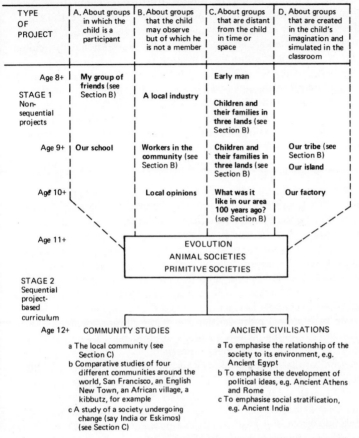

TYPE OF PROJECT	A. About groups in which the child is a participant	B. About groups that the child may observe but of which he is not a member	C. About groups that are distant from the child in time or space	D. About groups that are created in the child's imagination and simulated in the classroom
Age 8+ STAGE 1 Non-sequential projects	My group of friends (see Section B)	A local industry	Early man Children and their families in three lands (see Section B)	
Age 9+	Our school	Workers in the community (see Section B)	Children and their families in three lands (see Section B)	Our tribe (see Section B) Our island
Age 10+		Local opinions	What was it like in our area 100 years ago? (see Section B)	Our factory

Age 11+

EVOLUTION
ANIMAL SOCIETIES
PRIMITIVE SOCIETIES

STAGE 2
Sequential project-based curriculum

Age 12+ COMMUNITY STUDIES

a The local community (see Section C)
b Comparative studies of four different communities around the world, San Francisco, an English New Town, an African village, a kibbutz, for example
c A study of a society undergoing change (say India or Eskimos) (see Section C)

ANCIENT CIVILISATIONS

a To emphasise the relationship of the society to its environment, e.g. Ancient Egypt
b To emphasise the development of political ideas, e.g. Ancient Athens and Rome
c To emphasise social stratification, e.g. Ancient India

Source: D. Lawton *et al. Social Studies 8-13: Working Paper 39* (London, Evans), p. 156.

both of these emphases have helped history teachers to clarify their view of their subject. The final product of this project will be a series of handbooks but, until these become available, its *Interim Statement* and *Spotlights* (Blyth, 1972 and 1973) will be found very helpful.

INTERDISCIPLINARY COURSES 11-14
This age-band overlaps that of the 'middle years' but needs to be considered separately because some projects have been directed to secondary schools alone. Integration at this level has been particularly controversial because it has had to face the conventional commitment of the secondary school to the subject curriculum. In addition, the first attempt to develop a more flexible approach was promoted as a radical

innovation centred on the interests of the learner – the Inter-disciplinary Enquiry of the Goldsmiths' Curriculum Laboratory. As a result opinions became strongly polarised, the more so because the Laboratory never developed detailed strategies for structure, balance and sequence which are apparent in both the conventional curriculum and in all the major development projects.

The brief of the Schools Council Integrated Studies project was 'to examine the problems and possibilities of integrated studies in the humanities area of the curriculum' (1972: 5). It is interesting to reflect that 'problems' figure first – was this a backlash from IDE? The project has become known for its packs of materials, *Exploration Man, Communicating with Others* and *Living Together* and, as a result, the process of dissemination has perhaps obscured this original brief, but as Chart 14 illustrates, the project examined the rationale for integration in the humanities across the complete curriculum 10-18 (1972: 20). It realised that the case for any form of integrated approach at this level must depend upon identifying either some logical area of concern or natural grouping of subject disciplines. As the chart is examined in detail, it is interesting to see how little that is radical or revolutionary is being suggested – indeed in many schools only the second-year proposals (illustrated by the published packs) need cause any change. The other general concern of the project was to show that such changes would lead to changes in teacher role and school organisation: more flexible timetabling, more central use of the library, greater provision of resource materials and, most important, a willingness to co-operate between the teachers concerned.

Neither of the second level packs is directly based on history; the first, *Communicating with Others,* explores grouping in the area of the expressive arts and the other, *Living Together,* in that of the social studies. Nevertheless, in both packs the history teacher will find a clear and valuable role. For example, in *Communicating with Others,* he will not only participate in the study of the locality, in 'Look and Listen', but will also lead the 'Sense of History' unit. This deals with an outline of the development of writing and also studies two vital periods in the development of the English language – the Anglo-Saxon and Chaucerian.

The other type of integration being developed for this level is that where the course attempts to express a complete curriculum, as in *Man: A Course of Study.* This was inspired by Professor Bruner's interest in why we taught about man in his environment. His analysis led him to base the curriculum on three questions: 'What is human about human beings? How did they get that way? How can they be made more so?' So he argued, 'we should seek exercises and materials through which our pupils can learn wherein man is distinctive in his adaptation to the world, and wherein there is a discernible

Chart 14   INTEGRATION ACROSS THE CURRICULUM

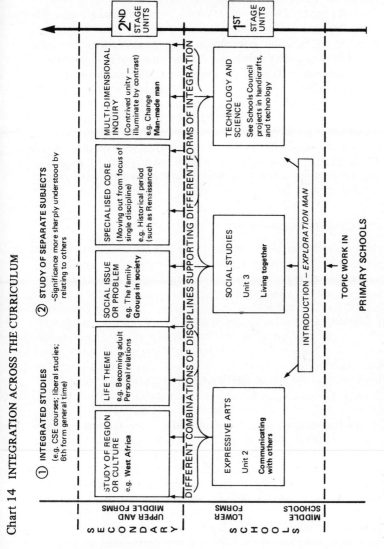

INTEGRATED STUDIES

2ND STAGE UNITS

1ST STAGE UNITS

① INTEGRATED STUDIES
(e.g. CSE courses; liberal studies; 6th form general time)

② STUDY OF SEPARATE SUBJECTS
−Significance more sharply understood by relating to others

STUDY OF REGION OR CULTURE
e.g. West Africa

LIFE THEME
e.g. Becoming adult Personal relations

SOCIAL ISSUE OR PROBLEM
e.g. The family **Groups in society**

SPECIALISED CORE
(Moving out from focus of single discipline)
e.g. Historical period (such as Renaissance)

MULTI-DIMENSIONAL INQUIRY
(Contrived unity − illuminate by contrast)
e.g. Change **Man-made man**

TECHNOLOGY AND SCIENCE
See Schools Council projects in handicrafts, and technology

EXPRESSIVE ARTS
Unit 2
Communicating with others

SOCIAL STUDIES
Unit 3
Living together

INTRODUCTION − *EXPLORATION MAN*

DIFFERENT COMBINATIONS OF DISCIPLINES SUPPORTING DIFFERENT FORMS OF INTEGRATION

UPPER AND MIDDLE FORMS
SECONDARY

LOWER FORMS
MIDDLE SCHOOLS

TOPIC WORK IN
PRIMARY SCHOOLS

Source: Schools Council Integrated Studies, *Introduction* (1972), p. 20.

continuity between him and his animal forbears' (1966: 74). The course is structured round what Bruner identified as the five great 'humanising' forces: tool-making, language, social organisation, child-rearing and man's urge to explain his world. These are expressed through a series of key concepts drawn from the social sciences: life cycle, innate and learned behaviour, adaptation, natural selection, structure and function, information and communication. (The other ways in which Bruner influenced the curriculum were to give it a spiral structure to optimise the understanding of such complex ideas and to base it on the evidence of social science field studies.[8])

Again, though the history teacher does not find his discipline directly represented, experience has shown that the evidential approach is well suited to his interests and that he has much to contribute on 'the urge to explain his world'. More important perhaps is the way in which the example of such a curriculum can help him to reconsider not only his approach to his own subject but the structure of the school curriculum as a whole.

INTEGRATED STUDIES 15-16

In the fourth and fifth years the pupils face the climax of two areas of preparation, for subject examinations and for the responsibilities of adulthood and citizenship. At present the number of integrated or inter-disciplinary examination syllabuses remain very few because of subject-based examinations. The four-subject, internally examined and moderated 'O' Level at Hedley Walter, Brentwood, remains almost unique.[9] By contrast, since the Newsom Report called for a radical re-appraisal of humanities teaching for the 'young school leaver', there has been an enormous expansion in the second area. It must be reiterated, however, that the aim of this development is primarily social: 'to develop understanding of human acts and social situations' (HCP, 1970: 8 or 'to develop a considerate style of life' (McPhail, 1969).

The Humanities Curriculum Project (HCP) was the first national humanities development project. At the same time it has become the most widely known of all such projects because of the controversy and publicity it has attracted. First, it asserted that the curriculum for this age/ability band must consist of 'significant human issues', of which it experimented with eight: war and society, relations between the sexes, poverty, living in cities, law and order, education, family, people and work (1970:6).[10] Even more controversial was its insistence that the logical method for realising this understanding must be discussion at the student's own level, so that the teacher became a 'neutral chairman'. Many teachers were disturbed because they saw this role as recessive. What was intended, however, was to argue for the primacy of being a consultant, indirectly controlling discussion through the selection of the issue and the provision of resources.

For these reasons the response evoked by the project has been very mixed. For history teachers, however, both its approach, the continual use of historical events as centres of discussion and enquiry, and its provision of rich packs of supporting material, offer tremendous opportunities. (There have been two other notable social education projects, those of the North-Western Region and the Liverpool Childwall project.[11] The HCP has been featured because it seems most directly useful to history teachers.)

16+ GENERAL STUDIES

Since the Crowther Report (1959) it has come to be accepted that the pattern of two or three 'A' Level subjects pursued in depth has both personal and social disadvantages as a structure for curriculum – a point of view recently restated in the Schools Council Working Papers 45 and 47.[12] There are two ways in which history teachers have been facing up to the criticisms voiced in these reports – the first of these is by widening the approach within their subject teaching, drawing upon a wider range of aspects in the way advocated by John Fines (see Chapters 2 and 3).

The other has been to exploit the freedom offered by General Studies. Crowther argued that the purpose of minority time was to 'complement' specialist studies, as by offering science for arts students, or to 'supplement' them by considerations of important but untreated areas such as ethics and morals. It was a fine ideal but one which suffered from being a minority concern and unexamined, and so reliant on the charismatic stimulus of the interested teacher. However, since then the foundation of the General Studies Association has given a great deal of strength to encouraging discussion and organising development. Its Project, financed by the Schools Council, tried not only to define a more specific rationale for such studies but, equally important, to provide teachers with the resources.

The criteria suggested by the Project were three: that the subject matter should be of 'significance' – about 'things that matter'; that teaching should aim to open up 'connections' between subjects; and, third, should try to encourage the 'transfer' of both skills and appropriate knowledge. The Project then set about collecting actual materials and topics that teachers had found useful in their teaching and, using its criteria together with the GILTS method (see p.66), organised them into collections for experimental use. As a result of the trials' experience the Project revised the collections for publication (Longmans–Penguin, 1972 on). Once again, both in method and in the content of the collections – and not only those on historical topics such as Nazi Germany – the history teacher can bring the human insights of history to support almost every aspect of the curriculum – in sum an expanding role.

CONCLUSION: OPPORTUNITY NOT SUBMERSION!

From all the examples above it should be obvious that no history teacher should feel despairing of his subject within any *properly planned* form of inter-disciplinary or integrated approach in the humanities.[13] The emphasis upon the use of evidence and the forming of critical judgement should surely satisfy any history teacher's concern for the value of his discipline. At the same time, the wider context offered by many of the frameworks, together with the greater opportunities for selection of content, should be directly helpful to those who urge wider aims for history teaching.

What the teacher has to be clear about are his objectives – oft-repeated but here more true than ever: David Bolam's article (1973b) makes this very clear and is also very helpful in its wealth of detailed practical illustration. The teacher who feels that he needs more understanding of 'integration' should turn to the articles by Richard Pring (1971), David Bolam (1971) and David Jenkins (1972). David Warwick's *Integrated Studies in the Secondary School* supplements these in its comparison of possible organisational structures, while both Lawton and Dufour (1973) and Mathias (1973) are extremely useful for their range of suggestions for practical syllabus making (but are both *social science* handbooks!). The present need, therefore, is to draw up precise objectives for *history* teaching – which is the concern of the next, and final, chapter.

NOTES

1. See Brooke quoted in Marwick (1970) *The Nature of History* (London, Macmillan).
2. Charity James (1968), *Young Lives at Stake* (London, Collins).
3. Portal adds the interesting remark that, while Americans have thought a great deal about rationales for 'Social Studies' and 'Life Adjustment' curricula, they lack the same kind of analysis for the more recent development of subject-based approaches.
4. See *Social Studies and the History Teacher* (London, Historical Association rev. edn 1967) and his chapter on interdisciplinary approaches in *Principles of History Teaching* (Methuen, 1971).
5. Now being examined by John Elliot in the Ford Foundation Project at CARE, University of East Anglia.

6. Recorded in Schools Council, Working Papers 22 and 42 (London, 1969; 1972).
7. Schools Council Environmental Studies Project *Case Studies* (London, Hart-Davis, 1972).
8. See Chart 8, p. 62. For his use of film see p. 90.
9. It is operated by the Associated Examining Board.
10. The ninth pack on Race Relations was unpublished.
11. The North West Regional Curriculum Development Project, *Social Education* (London, Macmillan, 1972-4); Liverpool Education Authority, *Childwall Project* (London, Arnold, 1972-3).
12. Schools Council, *16-19 Growth and Response, Working Paper 45: Curricular Bases* and *Working Paper 46: Examination Structure* (London, Evans, 1972 and 1973).
13. See Appendix 2.

BIBLIOGRAPHY

BLYTH, W.A.L. *et al.* (1972)*An Interim Statement* (London, Schools Council History, Geography and Social Science Project 8-13).
____ (1973) *Spotlights: A Summary of the Project's Approach* (London, Schools Council History, Geography and Social Science Project 8-13).
BOLAM, D. (1970-1) 'Integrating the Curriculum — A Case Study in the Humanities', in *Paedagogica Europaea,* vol. 6, pp.159-71.
____ (1973a) 'Teamwork to Launch Teamwork', in *Ideas*, no. 24, pp.16-25.
____ (1973b) 'History and Integrated Studies', in Jones (1973), pp. 256-85.
BRUNER, J.S. (1966) *Towards a Theory of Instruction* (Cambridge, Mass., Harvard).
BURSTON, W.H. and GREEN, C.W. (eds.) (1972) *Handbook for History Teachers* (London, Methuen, rev. edn).
EDUCATION DEVELOPMENT CENTER (1970) *Man: A Course of Study* (Washington, Curriculum Development Associates).
HUMANITIES CURRICULUM PROJECT(1970) *An Introduction* (London, Heinemann). See also collections: *Education, War and Society, Family, Relations between the Sexes, People and Work, Poverty, Law and Order, Living in Cities* (London, Heinemann, 1970-3).
JENKINS, D. (1972) 'The Integrated Studies Project', in *Curriculum Design and Implementation*, Unit 11, Course 283 (London, Open University), pp. 57-69.
JONES, R.B. (ed.) (1973) *Practical Approaches to the New History* (London, Hutchinson).
LAWTON, D. *et al.* (1971) *Social Studies 8-13: Working Paper 39* (London, Evans).
LAWTON, D. and DUFOUR, B. (1973) *New Social Studies* (London, Heinemann).
MATHIAS, P. (1973) *Social Studies Handbook* (London, Blandford).
McPHAIL, P. (1969) 'The Moral Education Curriculum Project', in C. Macy (ed.), *Let's Teach Them Right* (London, Pemberton).
PERRY, G. *et al.* (1971) *Environmental Studies* (London, Blandford).

PORTAL, C. (1972) 'The Place of History in Integrated and Interdisciplinary Studies', in Burston and Green (1972), pp. 114-25.

PRING, R. (1971) 'Curriculum Integration', in R. Hooper (ed.), *The Curriculum: Context, Design and Development* (Edinburgh, Oliver & Boyd), pp. 265-72.

SCHOOLS COUNCIL (1969) *General Studies 16-18, Working Paper* 25 (London, Evans).

——(1972) *Exploration Man: An Introduction to Integrated Studies* (Oxford, OUP).

——(1972) *Teacher's Guide to SCIS*, Units 2 and 3 (Oxford, OUP).

——(1973) *Environmental Studies: The Use of Historical Resources, Working Paper* 48 (London, Evans).

WARWICK, D. (1973) *Integrated Studies in the Secondary School* (London, ULP).

WATTS, D.C. (1967) *Environmental Studies* (London, Routledge).

Chapter 7

Towards the 'New' History:

an 'objectives' approach?

Teachers complained about the glibness of the theorists with their flood of advice and ideas about what should and should not be done, when what was really needed was immediate practical help to implement plans for syllabus reforms.

> History Teaching Today Group (1970) *The Teaching of History to the 11-14 Age Group* (Cambridge, Institute of Education), p. 17.

At some stage in every aspect of educational activity someone has to stand back and ask questions such as 'What are we doing?' 'How successful are we being?', and 'In what ways can we do better?' This can only be done if two things have happened.
1. That statements of what is being undertaken and of the objectives which it is hoped to achieve are in existence.
2. That these statements have been set down in writing so that others can read and discuss them.'

> Southern Regional Examining Board (n.d.) *Defining Objectives*, p.1.

The way in which teachers think about curriculum planning is an inversion of how the theorists think about it. For the theorist, curriculum planning usually starts by stating aims and objectives, the purposes the curriculum is to serve, and this is followed by a description of the learning experiences necessary to achieve the aims and objectives ... Teachers, on the other hand, appear to start understandably enough, with the context of teaching, follow this with a consideration of the kind of learning situation likely to interest and involve their pupils and only after this consider the purposes which their teaching is to serve. Lastly, and as an issue of lesser importance, teachers consider the criteria for a procedure for evaluating the effectiveness of their course of teaching.

> P.M. Taylor (1970) *How Teachers Plan Their Courses* (Slough), NFER), pp. 59-60.

No one who has lived through the last decade has been able to ignore the 'roaring current' of change. As Toffler argues, 'change is a process by which the future invades our lives' so that 'it is important to look at it closely, not merely from the grand perspectives of history but also from the advantage point of the living, breathing individuals who experience it'.[1] Not only education but history and history teaching have been, and are, undergoing such change. Yet many historians and history teachers have affected to ignore it. The aim of this short book has been ambitious, in setting out to help teachers survey all the dimensions of history teaching. But we hope that this will have shown: first, that the underlying trend is really one of logical evolution rather than of reaction and protest; and second, that its strands are clearly related and so convergent. The introduction opened on the much quoted note of pessimism: 'history in danger'. The conclusion hopes that teachers, drawing on the arguments we have reproduced, will become more optimistic — better able to confront change from within and without, with the confidence of anticipation.

The other introductory point to be made for this final chapter is that the purpose of the book altered as it progressed. Naturally, each chapter was designed to lead on to the next but, in the writing, each one began to end on a recurring note — the need for clearer and more specific definition of teaching objectives. The purpose of this final chapter is to examine what has been done in this field. The problem here was baldly stated in the HMI's survey: 'freshly conceived and thought out aims, stated in broad terms but closely geared to a comprehensive consideration of methods and teaching resources were scarcely to be found in a single syllabus' (Giles, 1973: 135). This is why this chapter opens with almost a page of quotations, which simply go to show the contrast in standpoints between teachers, examiners and educationists. The whole purpose of defining objectives is to bring these together.

OBJECTIVES: PROBLEMS AND DEFINITIONS

A teacher's main concern must be for his pupils. It is a demanding and exhausting task, so that the classroom is the natural focus of his working life — as Taylor's research has emphasised. The contemporary concern for motivation, however, must lead the teacher to include his subject. This concern is reflected in the main request made by the Cambridge-shire teachers for 'immediate, practical help with syllabus reform'. The previous chapters have shown the variety and ingenuity of response to this challenge, but the issue is whether such help is intended simply for the task of the lesson, for planning a patch or term's sequence of study, or for relating content and methods to the 'objectives' of teaching history? The root problem is this definition of objectives in teaching the subject.

What is really at issue is the interpretation being placed on the term 'objective'. As the Cambridge example illustrates, most history teachers still tend to use the word to describe a generalised aim or purpose. However, for the psychologist, the curriculum developer, and increasingly the examiner, the word is employed in a much more specific sense: ' "an educational objective", then, describes first what a *learner* can do as a result of having learned; and secondly, what an observer can see the learner doing so that he can judge whether or not the objective has been successfully reached. And thirdly, the objective, in describing what the learner will have achieved, also indicates what educational experience he requires if he is to achieve the objective' (Coltham and Fines, 1971: 3).

All this emphasis on objectives is also being made into a practical need by the changing character of examinations — as the previous chapter argues. The moves towards assessment, the acknowledgement that there is a range of areas to be examined, argue that any attempt at evaluation should have been closely related to initial syllabus design. This is the point being made in the second introductory quotation.

THE NEED FOR OBJECTIVES

(1) *Trends in curriculum reform*
'History teachers in general have so far shown themselves unwilling to provide statements of objectives', such is the view of Henry Mackintosh of the SREB (1973: 163). So it seems important to emphasise that the approach described in the previous paragraph has both a strong background of experience and general application. The Schools Council and the Inspectorate have done a great deal to publicise the approach during the last decade but it goes back much further. The seminal work is that of Tyler. His *Basic Principles of Curriculum and Instruction* is still seen as the classic statement, the attempt to balance the psychological claims of the child-centred 'progressive' movement with the 'essentialist' insistence on a knowledge-based curriculum. Tyler's contribution was to relate the 'ends' of essentialist instruction to the psychologically determined means, what is now termed the 'model-based' curriculum.

The other development was that initiated by Bloom for developing a 'theoretical framework which could be used to facilitate communication among examiners'. The importance of his much quoted *Taxonomy of Educational Objectives* was to refine earlier work into three categories, cognitive, affective and psycho-motor — all of which attempted to define teachers' aims in 'clear unambiguous terms describing the expected changes of behaviour'. Many teachers have found Bloom's analysis difficult to apply and Ebel's (1965) structure may appear an attractive alternative:

1. Understanding of terminology (or vocabulary)
2. Understanding of fact and principle (or generalisation)
3. Ability to explain or illustrate (understanding of relationships)
4. Ability to calculate (numerical problems)
5. Ability to predict (what is likely to happen under specified conditions)
6. Ability to recommend appropriate action (in some specific practical problem situation)
7. Ability to make an evaluative judgement.

(2) *Practical development*

The value of the leadership given by this American work is acknowledged in the succinct and cogent survey of *Curriculum Evaluation* by Wiseman and Pidgeon. The subject fields that have exemplified the approach most closely have been those of science and mathematics. These disciplines have the obvious advantage that their empirical and logical natures are ideally suited to an enquiry approach and that both appear to have a logical and hierarchical sequencing of concepts. In Britain the way in which these fields were suited to this approach has been demonstrated by the Nuffield science projects[2] which adopted this style and approach both in their general specifications and in their detailed programmes of work. There is little doubt that these projects can claim to have had a wide general effect: by 1971 Nuffield materials were being used in over 45 per cent of schools with GCE forms. At the same time the effect of this approach was widely felt in teacher education as a whole. The dimension in objectives which was initially undervalued was the 'affective' — 'the relation of science to society' and the development of a pupil's attitudes through the subject discipline. Here the current Science 5-13 Project under Ennever is an interesting example of the way the approach has subsequently been refined to show how the fostering of interests, attitudes and aesthetic awareness might be set against a staging of a Piagetian view of child development (see Appendix 3).

OBJECTIVES AND HISTORY TEACHING

It is against this background of experience and application that the apparently radical impact of the pamphlet *Educational Objectives for the Study of History* by Jeanette Coltham and John Fines needs to be considered. They have applied (see Chart 15) an analysis of the values of the subject taken from Bloom's original taxonomies and developed a framework under four heads: 'attitudes towards the study of history', 'nature of the discipline', 'skills and abilities' and 'educational

Chart 15 TWO TAXONOMIES COMPARED

(a) *Bloom*

History Content	**Pupil Behaviour**

1.0 *Historical Focus*
    1.1 Location
    1.2 Level of study
2.0 *Analysis over Time*
    2.1 Time periods
    2.2 Sequence
    2.3 Continuity and change
    2.4 Relationships
3.0 *Topical Emphasis*
    3.1 Political
    3.2 Social
    3.3 Economic
    3.4 Geographic
    3.5 Intellectual
    3.6 Cultural
4.0 *Methods of Inquiry*
    4.1 Evidence
    4.2 Verification
    4.3 Imagination
    4.4 Probability
    4.5 Interdisciplinary
        contributions
5.0 *Historiography*
6.0 *Historical Issues and*
    Interpretations
	Cognitive–Knowledge and
	Comprehension
	Facts
	Concepts
	Generalisations
	Structure and models
	Cognitive–Skills
	Location of information
	Interpretation of graphic and
	symbolic data
	Identification of central issues and
	assumptions
	Evaluation of evidence and drawing
	of warranted conclusions
	Formulation of reasonable
	hypotheses
	Group participation–formal
	Group participation–informal
	Affective–Attitudes and Values
	Scientific approach to human
	behaviour
	Humanitarian outlook on the
	behaviour of others
	Awareness and interest
	Acceptance of responsibility
	Involvement
	Democratic values

(b) *Coltham and Fines*

A. *Attitudes towards the Study*
   of History
   1. Attending
   2. Responding
   3. Imagining
B. *Nature of the Discipline*
   1. Nature of the information
   a) primary sources
   b) secondary sources
   2. Organising procedures
   3. Products
	C. *Skills and Abilities*
	   1. Vocabulary acquisition
	   2. Reference skills
	   3. Memorisation
	   4. Comprehension
	   5. Translation
	   6. Analysis
	   7. Extrapolation
	   8. Synthesis
	   9. Judgement and evaluation
	  10. Communication skills
	D. *Educational Outcomes of Study*
	   1. Insight
	   2. Knowledge of values
	   3. Reasoned judgement

Source: Phyllis Giles and G. Neal (1973) 'History Teaching Analysed', in *Trends in Education*, no. 32, p. 17.

outcomes'. As can be seen from the chart, these major categories are then broken down into subheadings, which in turn subsume a range of very precise objectives. For instance, B1, the 'nature of information', moves from the evaluation of source material in terms of authenticity, relevance, coherence and reliability, to the recognition of gaps in the evidence, to distinguishing between primary and secondary material, to the detection of bias and the separation of fact from value judgement, to end in the synthesis of 'materials culled from more than one source' (1971: 13).

There is no doubt that this type of approach is extremely demanding; not only does it ask for a great deal of preliminary work on structure but a proper evaluation can only be achieved by applying it to specific tasks or situations. Furthermore, few teachers are yet familiar with this style of analysis and its language. Not surprisingly therefore, the initial reaction was frequently hostile, particularly because some assumed the framework to be prescriptive – a general model to which all history teaching must conform. However, this was simply to misunderstand the authors' purpose. First, their expressed aim was simply to encourage thinking and discussion as implied by the word 'suggested' in their sub-title. Secondly, the purpose of a taxonomy is still widely misunderstood. Henry Mackintosh has emphasised again and again that it is an 'essential piece of starting equipment but *only* that'. Its main purpose is to help clarify the design and evaluation of syllabuses.

This point is well brought out in a typically thorough and interesting analysis of the use of taxonomies as frameworks for history teaching by two HMIs, Giles and Neal (1974). The general theme of their argument is that such frameworks are badly needed, but their critical comments are worth noting, particularly because they can be compared with the practical experience of Roberts (1973), who applied Coltham and Fines in order to analyse the teaching of the 'O' level syllabus taken by his school. First, the HMIs felt that the analysis appeared to concentrate too much on cognitive skills and that it could be argued as applicable to almost any discipline, thus leaving aside the question of what is particular to the historical way of thinking. The point that Roberts makes is that even a cursory analysis of his syllabus showed that the examination seemed confined to category C and, of the ten possible skills, encouraged only four (memorisation, synthesis, analysis and communication). So the taxonomy was helpful in enabling his team to enlarge their perception of their teaching. Of course, if misapplied, such a framework could create a 'mechanistic' approach stressing knowledge of concepts at the expense of wider understanding.

On the 'affective' side, the development of values, Giles and Neal like the way in which the Coltham-Fines framework did not include precise goals like 'democratic values' as did Bloom, but then they suggest that it was too 'imprecise'! Again it is interesting to see how Roberts interpreted this area. He discerned three ends: 'to find history an interesting and life-enriching subject'; 'to motivate the pupils to develop their own special interests' in it and to 'encourage an historical imagination'. His realisation that these were necessarily long-term goals, that specific opportunities would need to be provided to stimulate their realisation, together with the sensible reservation that there were 'many snags still to be overcome', perhaps goes much of the way to meet the reservations of the HMIs. His conclusion is, however, undeniably optimistic: 'The process of developing it [the approach] has convinced us that the educational objectives approach is a fruitful one which may enable anyone not only to improve his existing course but also to devise methods of assessment which enhance rather than distort his classwork' (1973: 125).

CONCLUSION: A LOOK TO THE FUTURE

The English dislike revolutions! Although the objectives approach can make claims to a tradition and has now won some acceptance, it may well appear too radical or 'mechanistic' to many. Perhaps this was the problem that Nisbet visualised when, as long ago as 1957, he brought up the question of the 'extensive but ill-charted intermediate area of thought which lies between general abstract aims on the one hand and highly specific (classroom) aims on the other'. He concluded that there was the need for 'practical, intermediate objectives'. This is where Roberts' interpretation of the 'framework' appeared to us a helpful conclusion to this final chapter — an attractive example of just such an approach. It is practical in applying the approach to a specific need and intermediate in that the case was an example of a more general issue. The extensions to these points also seem important to bring out: firstly, that adopting the approach was seen as developmental both for the 'O' level course and the school syllabus; and secondly, and more important, that the example reflected the ideas and feelings of a team rather than the individual teacher described by Nisbet.

Hoyle's 'extended professionalism' is altogether too weighty a moral for this short book. Perhaps Alice put it more simply:

'Would you tell me please, which way I ought to go from here?'
'That depends a good deal on where you want to get to,' said the Cat.
'I don't much care where . . . ,' said Alice.
'Then it doesn't matter which way you go,' said the Cat.
'. . . so long as I get somewhere!, Alice added as an explanation.

Perhaps her only mistake was to explore alone? If Hoyle's road is a hard one it need not be a lonely one!

NOTES

1. See A. Toffler (1970) *The Future Shock* (Harmondsworth, Pan Books) p. 11.
2. 1966 onwards.

BIBLIOGRAPHY

BLOOM, B.S. *et al.* (1954) *Taxonomy of Educational Objectives. The Classification of Educational Goals*, Handbook 1: *Cognitive Domain* (Harlow, Longmans).
——(1971) *Handbook on Formative and Summative Evaluation of Student Learning* (New York, McGraw-Hill).
COLTHAM, Jeanette B. and FINES, J. (1971) *Educational Objectives for the Study of History* (London, Historical Association).
EBEL, R.L. (1965) *Measuring Educational Achievement* (New York, Prentice-Hall).
EISNER, E.W. (1967) 'Educational Objectives: Help or Hindrance?', *The School Review*, vol. 75, no. 3, pp. 250-60.
FENTON, E. (1966) *Teaching the New Social Studies in Secondary Schools* (New York, Holt, Rinehart & Winston), pp. 19-96.
GILES, Phyllis (1973) 'History in the Secondary School: A Survey', in *Journal of Curriculum Studies*, vol. 5, pp. 133-44.
GILES, Phyllis and NEAL, G. (1973) 'History Teaching Analysed', in *Trends in Education*, no. 32, pp. 16-25.
GRIBBLE, J.H. (1970) 'Pandora's Box: The Affective Domain of Educational Objectives', in *Journal of Curriculum Studies*, vol. 2, no. 1, pp. 11-24.
GRONLUND, N.E. (1970) *Stating Behavioural Objectives in the Classroom* (London, Macmillan).
HOGBEN, D. (1972) 'The Behavioural Objectives Approach: Some Problems and Some Dangers', in *Journal of Curriculum Studies*, vol. 4, no. 1, pp. 42-50.
JONES, R.B. (ed.) (1973) *Practical Approaches to the New History* (London, Hutchinson).
LAWTON, D. and DUFOUR, B. (1973) *New Social Studies* (London, Heinemann).
MACINTOSH, H.G. (1973) 'Assessment at Sixteen-Plus in History', in Jones (1973), pp. 161-95.
MUSGROVE, F. (1968) 'Curriculum Objectives', in *Journal of Curriculum Studies*, vol. 1, no. 1, pp. 5-18.
NISBET, S. (1957) *Purpose in the Curriculum* (London, ULP).
ROBERTS, M. (1973) 'A Different Approach to O-Level', in Jones (1973), pp. 109-31.

SCHOOLS COUNCIL (1972) *With Objectives in Mind, Guide to Science 5-13* (London, Macdonald).

STENHOUSE, L. (1970-1) 'Some Limitations of the Use of Objectives in Curriculum Research and Planning', in *Paedagogica Europaea*, vol. 6, pp. 73-83.

SOUTHERN UNIVERSITY REGIONAL EXAMINATIONS BOARD (n.d.) *Defining Objectives* (cyclostyled).

TABA, Hilda (1962) *Curriculum Development: Theory and Practice* (New York, Harcourt, Brace & World).

TYLER, R.W. (1949) *Basic Principles of Curriculum and Instruction* (Chicago, Ill., Univ. of Chicago Press).

WISEMAN, S. and PIDGEON, D. (1970) *Curriculum Evaluation* (NFER).

Appendix 1
Four suggested world history frameworks

WORLD HISTORY SYLLABUS 1: CHRONOLOGICAL APPROACH

This syllabus takes chronological stages of development, illustrated by selected examples. Many examples are given, but it is not expected that more than two or three would be tackled in a term.

Year 1 Man learns to live in society
(a) extinct prehistoric cultures from the Stone, Bronze and Iron Ages, and possibly some recent primitive cultures such as Eskimo, Maoris, Negro African villages.
(b) early literate civilisations such as the Egyptian, Sumerian, Indus Valley, Yellow River, Mayan cultures.
(c) foundation of European civilisation in Classical Greece and Rome.

Year 2 Pre-industrial civilisations
(a) classical Hindu India.
(b) Tang or Sung China.
(c) the Mayas or the Incas
(d) Islamic culture in eleventh or twelfth centuries.
(e) European Christendom in the thirteenth century.
(f) one African kingdom such as Ghana, Mali or Ethiopia.

Year 3 Background to the present day
(a) British or Western European and/or American scientific and industrial development and its social and economic consequences.
(b) the political and economic development of a communist society.
(c) the progress of a developing nation under imperialism and under independence.
(d) world conflict and co-operation in the twentieth century.

WORLD HISTORY SYLLABUS 2 : AREA APPROACH

This syllabus gives the opportunity to put history in its geographical setting. Therefore at the start of each study the geographical background and the economic resources would be studied, and would be kept in mind throughout as part of the reason for the development or lack of development of an area at any particular stage of its history. Progress through the syllabus is from the more familiar areas to the less familiar.

Year 1
(a) *Britain and Western Europe:* formation of nation states, expansion of Europe, industrialisation, imperialism, European culture, decline of Europe in the twentieth century.
(b) *United States:* formation of the United States, industrialisation, American culture, America as a world power.

Year 2

(a)*India:* age of classical Hinduism, Muslim period, British occupation, social and political problems of independence;

either

(b)*Arab world in the Middle East or North Africa:* foundations and spread of Islam, cultural peak, commercial expansion and decline, modern Arab nationalism.

or

(c)*Sample areas of Africa south of the Sahara:* Negro kingdoms, European occupation, social and political problems of independent African nations.

Year 3

(a) *Russia:* social and political organisation of Imperial Russia in the nineteenth century, revolutions of 1917, social and political organisation and culture of Soviet Union.

(b)*China or Japan:* social and political organisation in the imperial age, effect of European impact, political and economic development in the twentieth century.

WORLD HISTORY SYLLABUS 3: THEMATIC APPROACH

This syllabus allows for the detailed development through the ages of a variety of themes, each taken on a broad front. Choice would have to be made from the examples offered.

Year 1 Man's need for food

(a) primitive and prehistoric food-gathering communities.

(b)the beginnings of settled agriculture.

(c)developments of more advanced techniques: irrigation, traction animals; problems of famine.

(d)twentieth-century agriculture: mechanisation, collectivisation, improved crops, fertilisation, international attempts to prevent starvation and soil erosion.

Year 2 People in cities

(a) ancient cities in classical Europe, India or China.

(b)capital cities of European nation states.

(c)the first industrial cities of Western Europe and America.

(d)new twentieth century cities in the Soviet Union, Latin America and Africa.

Year 3 Government

(a)varieties of early forms of government: Athenian democracy, Roman republic, Chinese or Indian Empire, tribal rule in Africa, European monarchy.

(b)development of complex forms of government over large numbers of people in the modern world, e.g. British Empire and Commonwealth, United States, Soviet Union.

(c)development of world government: League of Nations, United Nations.

WORLD HISTORY SYLLABUS 4 : COMPARATIVE APPROACH

This syllabus gives the opportunity of comparing and contrasting
significant aspects of development in different areas of the world.
It starts with the easier concepts likely to be within the pupils'
experience, and moves towards the more difficult. Each term it
may be necessary to start with some definitions in terms of what
pupils already know of their own country, in order to find points
of reference for comparison with other areas. The main work is on
the other areas of the world. These might be chosen from the following:
China, India, Japan, Negro Africa, the Arab world, Latin America. The
number of areas chosen would depend on the ability of the pupils.

Year 1
(a) traditional family and class organisation: authority of head of family
upbringing of children, marriage customs, position of women,
relationship of class to work, social mobility, differences in rich and
poor.
(b) changes made in traditional structures by colonialism, industrialisation
and modern nationalism.

Year 2
(a) the peasant in traditional society and in the twentieth century: old
and new relationships with the landlord, old and new techniques
and crops.
(b) cities and commerce in the past and in the twentieth century.
(c) technology and industry in traditional societies and since the
industrial revolution: e.g. iron and steel, textiles, pottery.

Year 3
(a) belief and its effects on way of life and on customs at birth,
marriage and death.
(b) government: a comparison of ancient empires such as the Han and
the Roman; a comparison of republican governments such as the
French and American; a comparison of communist government in
the Soviet Union and China; problems of world government.

Source: Islay Doncaster (unpublished).

Appendix 2
An integrated syllabus
for the lower secondary school

A teacher-designed syllabus, incorporating an enquiry-based evidential approach within a structured sequential framework.

YEAR 1

Unit 1 An island
The first three sections introduce the pupils to the components of the physical environment by involving them in creating by stages that of an imaginary volcanic island. The fourth section introduces the essential basis for the rest of the course in the problem of human group survival. The unit introduces the pupils to enquiry methods and is also designed to exercise their constructive and imaginative thinking.

Unit 2 Primitive life
The aim of this unit is to introduce the children to the study of human culture through studies of simple societies – the Eskimo, Aborigines, Bushmen and Tribes of New Guinea.

It introduces methods of studying societies and the kinds of questions to ask about them.

The unit uses a varied selection of material and evidence for investigation – filmstrips, slides, tapes, 'eye-witness' accounts, anthropologists' reports and myths and legends.

The unit lends itself to a great deal of creative work and to the discussion of important ideas about Man and his behaviour.

Unit 3 Man in the Stone Age
The aim of this unit is to show the progress of Man through the Stone Age and so to develop the studies in Unit 2 at the same time as introducing the problems of historical understanding.

The main skills involved are obtaining information from actual artefacts, paintings and human remains, making 3-D models or drawing cross-sections from contour maps.

YEAR 2

Unit 4 Ancient civilisations
This occupies the first term of the second year.

The aim of the unit is to investigate ways of life which are generally accepted as being civilised. It is a comparative study with the ancient civilisations of Mesopotamia, Egypt, Greece and Rome forming the core of the investigations.

The skills established during the preceding units are reinforced and extended during this course. As with successive units, at this stage more freedom is allowed for individual investigations of topics of interest associated with the theme.

Much interesting work is done during this unit based on the rich sources of myth and legend of these civilisations.

The unit also provides opportunities for dealing with the historical facts of the life of Christ, as well as discussion about the ideas he introduced.

Problems concerned with law and order are also raised in this unit.

Unit 5 Exploration
This unit is concerned with Man as an explorer and adventurer, seeking out new realms and new knowledge.

Unit 6 An environmental study
This may vary from year to year. At present a scheme is being used which involves an historical, sociological and geographical investigation of Kidlington and develops such skills as mapping, drawing up questionnaires, interviewing and the collation of a vast range of factual information. The children are then posed the problem of attracting to Kidlington 2,000 people and then of planning for their accommodation. It is very challenging, but in this day and age, a very pertinent study.

YEAR 3

Unit 7–8 America: Features of the study
This study is designed to last two terms. It is made up of units of materials prepared by the Nuffield Resources for Learning team.

Unit 9 World problems
This involves studies which spotlight problems such as hunger, poverty, disease, illiteracy, overpopulation, pollution, conservation, the pressures of living in large cities etc. The emphasis may change from year to year.

During the third year the nature of geography and history as separate disciplines are examined in order to help children when they come to choosing their GCE or CSE examination courses.

Source: C. Pack, Humanities at Gosford Hill School, Kidlington, Oxfordshire (unpublished).

Appendix 3
Affective objectives in Science 5-13 (an extract)

What we mean by Stage 1, Stage 2 and Stage 3

Stage 3
Transition to stage of abstract thinking.

This is the stage in which, for some children, the ability to think about abstractions is developing. When this development is complete their thought is capable of dealing with the possible and hypothetical, and is not tied to the concrete and to the here and now. It may take place between eleven and thirteen for some able children, for some children it may happen later, and for others it may never occur. The objectives of this stage are ones which involve development of ability to use hypothetical reasoning and to separate and combine variables in a systematic way. They are appropriate to those who have achieved most of the Stage 2 objectives and who now show signs of ability to manipulate mentally ideas and propositions.

Attitudes, interests and aesthetic awareness
.00/.10

3.11 Appreciation of the main principles in the care of living things.
3.12 Willingness to extend methods used in science activities to other fields of experience.

Attitudes, interests and aesthetic awareness
.00/.10

3.01 Acceptance of responsibility for their own and others' safety in experiments.
3.02 Preference for using words correctly.
3.03 Commitment to the idea of physical cause and effect.
3.04 Recognition of the need to standardise measurements.
3.05 Willingness to examine evidence critically.
3.06 Willingness to consider beforehand the usefulness of the results from a possible experiment.
3.07 Preference for choosing the most appropriate means of expressing results or observations.
3.08 Recognition of the need to acquire new skills.
3.09 Willingness to consider the role of science in everyday life.

Observing, exploring and ordering observations
.20

3.21 Appreciation that classification criteria are arbitrary.
3.22 Ability to distinguish observations which are relevant to the solution of a problem from those which are not.
3.23 Ability to estimate the order of magnitude of physical quantities.

Reproduced by permission of the Schools Council from *With Objectives in Mind*, prepared by the Science 5-13 Project, published by Macdonald Educational 1972, pp. 60-1.

Appendix 4
Objectives in teaching history at the university

Objectives: Skills	Activities	Evaluation
Undertaking a university history course should enable the student:		Essays show development of critical and analytic faculties (or lack of it). Otherwise evaluation entirely by examination
1. to ask productive questions, 2. to evaluate evidence, 3. to locate problems in their social and political context,	essays, based on reading original documents, articles, monographs, etc. illustrated in lectures and articles; essay writing	
4. to isolate 'causal factors of change', 5. to predict the outcome or development of a particular situation, 6. to deal with problems of communication, by ordering thoughts and presenting facts logically, 7. to argue effectively,	essays, tutorials, discussions; answering questions	
8. to recognise logically-ordered arguments based on reasonable facts, 9. to criticise others' arguments and presentation, 10. to build up complete pictures of historical situations, selecting their most important aspects, 11. to embark upon analysis of *any* social situation – topical, political or historical.	reading recent articles, etc., as well as historical ones tutorials, seminars	

Appendix 4 continued

Objectives in teaching history at the university

Knowledge and understanding | *Corresponding activities*

History teaching should help the student towards:

1. an understanding of the methodology of history,

2. a knowledge of the past, together with an ability to extend it,

3. an awareness that context is more important than facts, which only assume significance through their location within a situation,

4. an understanding of social and cultural influences on historical occurrences.

Corresponding activities

illustrated in lectures and historians' books and articles

all parts of course: background reading

Attitudes

History teaching should aim to foster in the student:

1. an appreciation of the art of analysis,

2. an 'historical attitude', so that he thinks in historical terms,

3. an appreciation of the different aspects of the society in which he lives,

4. an awareness of the changes already made in human society, and of those in progress.

all parts of course: the example of historians at work in the department

Source: Ruth Beard (1970) *Teaching and Learning in Higher Education* (Harmondsworth, Penguin), pp. 75-6.

Index

PART 2 AUTHORS

DATE DUE			
MR 1 '77			
OC 11 77			

Chaffer 155381